3 Musketeers of Evil

John Fowler

In loving memory of (Face) Bill and Doris Fowler, who had to be the original inspiration for the TV show "All in the Family."

I love you Mose.

Forward, Onward and Upward

This book is dedicated to you, the reader. The words within are best explained by the energy potential of the 3 Musketeers of Evil. The human brain is very complex and uniquely capable of thoughts beyond our imagination. I guess we all have a compartment inside of that grey matter of the brain reserved for the analytical mind searching innovative ideas, humor, or having a zany side hidden away and not usually shared with the world. The human brain is home to 87 billion neurons and has no room for the 3 Musketeers of Evil but the disease flourishes in the minds of many. This book is the work of my alter ego, fellow Epistemologist Josephus Flavius Solo. He's been around a long time and has seen or experienced a plethora of life's conundrums. Whether you find him moronic of mind or not will be evident in the contents of this book. You may find he needs a chill pill and you may feel certain he's certifiably crazy. While I may agree with you, I have finally relented to this inward desire to tell the world just how he feels, replete with a plethora of subjects that he really thinks he has the logical answers to. Due diligence and research for the truth will lead one to an infinite biased solution to the fear, pestilence and panic of the world's problems we are faced with today. America and the rest of the world has been stricken with a terminal moronic disease of evil and the future looks bleak. For more "bleak news" the mind of J. Flavius Solo will begin his reasoning right after you turn this page. J. Flavius is about to share those hidden away thoughts, opinions and logic in print for you to read. It is a fact the true resident mind of Josephus is not a real person. He still lingers around in the mind of its truest author and resident sponsorship of W. John Fowler, however I take no personal responsibility for most of its contents or subject matter. J. Flavius Solo is the very person you need to complain to at josephusflaviussolo@gmail. com. Flavius is older in his years and has an overtly biased abstract opinion of just about every subject known to mankind. He is driven by the world in all of its confusion, and sees America and the vicissitudes of life and the world's problems differently. The Mind of J. Flavius Solo is overwhelmed with the following basics: Is there really a better way to do things? Does logic ever take precedence? Can energy ever become free? Can we survive in a world of such crime, prejudice and turmoil? Are there really UFO's? Is God ubiquitous? Read on my friends as you peruse the mind of Josephus Flavius Solo! I would only ask that you ponder on the contents of each story as that of a visionary, by contemplating innovative ideas or new concepts and new visions you may have and want to share. Some topics will not agree with your thinking or knowledge, so the challenge is to reason with me and please, don't hesitate to contact Mr. Solo anytime: josephusflaviussolo@gmail.com

American citizens need to strive to become a nation of researchers who know the truth. Most researchers already know the meaning of real truth as clearly as the "writing on the wall" as was seen and interpreted by the prophet Daniel. Our planet is immersed, doomed and dumbed down by lies and deception. But for now, I too, will sit back and read this book once again. Suffice it to say that I am not sure if it was written just for me, or the book was intended for you to read. I can only hope we all get something out of this effort, but if even one person becomes illuminated by the reading of this book and is able to ferret out the true identity of our creator, I have completed the mission. While the 3 Musketeers of Evil seek to consume and destroy the souls of mankind there are 3 Musketeers of Good who will destroy evil once and for all, suspended in eternity.

TABLE OF CONTENTS

Chapter 1

———✦———

ELIMINATE NATIONAL DEBT 101 AND MAC'S BIG FANNIE

FACT: Our national debt is so high that if we raised $168 million dollars a day for 150 years, it still wouldn't pay back the debt!

CASE IN POINT: The old adage of the Fox watching the Henhouse is alive and prolifically well in Washington.

DISCUSSION: Around 1776, the people of America bought $28 million dollars worth of government bonds to fund the American Revolution. When the Civil War came along, Americans stepped up to the plate again. When the Spanish-American War and World War I ensued, Americans bought government bonds. In fact, the Louisiana Purchase, the Panama Canal and the first transcontinental railroad was funded (paid in full), by purchase of government bonds.

In 1941, the government offered Defense Stamps and Defense Bonds and changed the name of these bonds to War Bonds after the attack on Pearl Harbor. Between 1941 and 1945, this great nation and the people of the United States raised $55 billion dollars, with a pride of having financed the entire war effort and equally participated in an important victory.

So, what happened with the government using a Savings Bond System that was focused on a single purpose as the example of saving up money for impending wars, making the Louisiana Purchase, paying all of the debt for the Panama Canal Project and paying all of the debt for the Trans-continental Railroad? Is there something wrong with my way of thinking or am I just old fashioned, senile and out of touch with the pulse of common sense? Does it appear that by selling bonds, the government used this program to "pay the debt incurred in full" for certain projects and efforts? My question is "what did congress do with all of the unspent bond money? Was it absorbed into another bond or hidden away for the congressional picky pockets? It sure as hell wasn't used to pay back the U.S. veterans known as the "Bonus Vets" after WWI.

Who sold out the American people by printing money that has no backing? Then, after facing a terrible congress caused debt because of Fannie Mae and Freddie Mac, we ended up borrowing over a trillion dollars from China? Who would of thought China had the money to bail the United States out of debt? China was nearly devastated and crushed by the Japanese during WWII. The United States came to their aid and we fought with Chinese soldiers against Japan. Seventy years later, China has become so productive they own $1.712 trillion dollars in American U.S. Treasury Bonds and NOT the American people. By the way, our second biggest banker is that little country of Japan who owns $1.197 trillion dollars of American U.S. Treasury Bonds. While Spanish seems to be our second language here in the United States, we might want to freshen up on speaking Mandarin Chinese or Japanese.

J. SOLO'S SOLUTION: Bonds. Let's call them "Specific Purpose Bonds", as we did before we entered into WW II. Back then we called them War Bonds. If the use of Specific Purpose Bonds were enacted, it will only be available to American Citizens and not China or Japan or any other foreign country. Americans can and should take care of their own problems.

Bonds have been around for a long time. In 1914, Germany sold bonds with a 5% return. Not bad for 1914, huh? Canada's "Victory Bonds" in 1918, gave a 5.5% return. The British sold "Exchequer Bonds" in 1918, with a 5% return. In 1917 and 1918, the United States sold "Liberty Bonds", and even the Boy and Girl Scouts of America sold them under the slogan "Every Scout to Save a Soldier." During WWII, Canada sold bonds in February 1940, and met its goal of $20 million in 48 hours. In September, Canada's Second Issue in 1940, sold another $30 million, reaching its goal almost as quickly. Over the course of WWII, 85 million Americans purchased "War Bonds" totaling nearly $185 billion dollars. I want to camp on this thought and reiterate the following facts:

Most wars fought by Americans, were purchased as bonds, bought by Americans for that specific purpose, and nearly all wars in the recent history of America were paid for by the American Bond Program. The Panama Canal Project was paid for by Americans through the Bond Program.

The Panama Canal Project was paid for in full by Americans who purchased Bonds.

The Louisiana Purchase was paid for by Americans who purchased Bonds. The Transcontinental Railroad was paid for through purchase of the Bonds.

When the debt of Fannie Mae and Freddie Mac was exposed, the government needed a ton of money outside of our normal budget. Our president should have told the American people how much debt was incurred and immediately offered not Defense Bonds, but "Specific Purpose Bonds" that would pay off that specific debt, with a promise that Fannie May and Freddie heads would roll and the political jesters of greed would spend a little time in jail. Well, nobody "rolled" except the crime committed and no one was held accountable and the jesters are still dancing in their greed. Congress had their dirty hands all over that mess and so did a lot of others, and no one went to jail. In the meantime, our government ran to China for a loan, which us American People will have to pay for. While we are constantly reminded to buy American, America needs to learn how to take care of its own problems before kneeling at the foot of a Communist country begging like a whore-dog for alms. The Fannie Mae and Freddie Mac mess could have been paid off by American citizens, who purchased "Specific Purpose Bonds." Not China.

For Example: If I purchased $10 thousand dollars worth of Fannie Mae and Freddie Mac Specific Purpose Bonds, I now own a part of that company. As holder of the Fannie Mae and Freddie Mac Bonds, this entitles me to a percentage of monetary royalties, as long as I hold onto my bonds. When the Fannie Mae and Freddie Mac Bond effort begins to make a profit, I will begin making a profit as an investor. This same methodology could be applied to many of the money blunders this country gets itself into. Each time the president or congress needs extra money for issues outside of the government's budget, it should be acquired in the form of a "Specific Purpose Bond" designated for that particular cause. It probably wouldn't take long before the president and congress went hog wild trying to cash in these Specific Purpose Bonds for a different purpose, but you and I would still have the power to vote these people out of office as quickly as they got in. If you're looking for a blatant example of the term "Hog Wild", take a look at the millions and millions of dollars congress has been stealing from our Social Security System. Let's begin investing in America again and keep our debts at home and paid in full by American Citizens. What are politicians thinking when this great nation has to cower before China and Japan and beg for more money?

Is America still using the Bond System? Yes. Bond sales continued after WWII. Non-Specific sales of Bonds have been purchased by Americans from 1946, and continues to this day, and that seems to be part of the problem. We have no audit trail of where the unused bond money went afterwards, (we must have authorized congress to make those decisions for us – well, yes they did and there is the systemic problem). While there are specific "College" Bonds you can purchase, one can only imagine what the Washington D. C. foxes and chickens are doing with all of the rest of the Non-Specific, Non-Designated Bond henhouse money?

CLOSING THOUGHT: It doesn't cost a thing to pay attention. Notice the War Bond picture below and camp on the word "Americans." American Citizens purchased those War Bonds. Not China, not Japan, no foreign entity except Americans, taking on its own problems and funding its own needs.

Let's again hypothetically assume we now have a new bond program called Specific Purpose Bond. An example would be a bond known as "SPB Feed Our Children." Whoever manages this bond program will be an honest congressman, (God help us). No American Congressman or woman or president can authorize funds to be taken out of that specific bond for any other purpose without the American bond owners' written permission. How about if we were to introduce other bonds known as "SPB The Homeless Problem" and "SPB Disaster Relief" or "SPB Stop Crime." Imagine if the American people invested in bonds to stop crime? Every normal person in America would invest in this program. I'm not looking for utopia here, but think what that kind of money could do to slow crime in America down to a crawl? Do we have any idea what our "return on investment" would be? I'm thinking of living in a safe America again. Oh, and us bondholders of "SPB Stop Crime" will be worth a boatload of money as crime diminishes. Our efforts would provide a safe country to live in and we could reap the profits, not the politics of Congress.

The creation of humanity began with one person. If every single person believed in a worthy cause to stand up for, this might be a good starting point. And me? I'm all in. In fact, I am writing a letter to the governor of California and do everything I can do to propose a Specific Purpose Bond program that will stop crime in California. How about a crime free Congress? It's amazing what us Americans can do when it starts with honesty. Imagine the value added.

josephusflaviussolo@gmail.com

Chapter 2

WE DON'T NEED YOUR MIDDLE EASTERN OIL

FACT: America is dependent on foreign oil.

American money is not going to purchase oil from countries that
hate us.
Uncle Sam's handout money will no longer be available to hostile
countries.

CASE IN POINT: So, the President of Venezuela hates us? Let's
have a "Shove Your Well Up Your Gas-hole" campaign? How about
a whole bunch of shove it campaigns and demonstrate to the OPEC
middle eastern oil mongers some real American authority. By the way,
the United States approved a loan to Venezuela culminating in $55 bil-
lion dollars that you and I will never see the debt paid in return. The
Venezuelan government hates us, but love our money. Do we American
Citizens have a voice in this government of ours other than voting?

I don't remember being asked about loaning all of that money to a country whose president hates the United States? I don't remember authorizing our government to borrow $1.7 trillion dollars from China, and I don't recall ever voting to give money away to foreign nations that hate America. Oh, that's right. I checked and found out that I did vote. I voted for what I thought were honest faithful representatives as governors, presidents, congressmen and congresswomen just like you did. Just like you, I placed loyalty, honesty and integrity in government representatives, believing that America would conduct business logically on my behalf. We all know that no one in their right mind would buy their oil and supply a Middle Eastern country with U.S. made weapons and have those same weapons used against us, right? Research the Web and learn how many hostile countries we give free money to every year. I'll bet one of those "'ran" countries we give money to are still calling us Americans' the "Nation of the Great Satan" before they even get to the bank to cash one of dear ol' Uncle Sam's free handouts. These and other countries hostile towards America take great delight in killing our American citizens, but as soon as Uncle Sam approaches, they bow in adoration, waiting for the next free monetary handout. Of course, America, Big Brother of the World, doesn't feel the kick in the pants or the knife in our back after thinking we made peace with our money. In the meantime us Americans have to bow down also, because somehow, we have become dependent on foreign oil and it is you and me that bears the responsibility.

DISCUSSION: There must be a better way. If I had a relative or an adult child constantly reaching into my back pocket, I can guarantee you it wouldn't take long before I decided enough was enough. There seems to be a plague going on in this generation that feels mom and dad has money and kids and relatives need to live off of it too. We all know a plethora of these cases going on all around us. "Tough Love" seems to work. While there are exceptions, we need to help these relatives and adult children understand the words work and retirement are more important than lazy and irresponsible. Can "Tough Love" be applied to those countries that hate us? Can "Tough Love" be applied to those countries that hold us hostage for their oil?

J. SOLO'S SOLUTION: There are two problems we need to consider in this discussion. The Oil Problem in America and those countries that hate America.

Problem #1: The Oil Problem In America. How about this idea: "As of this date, whatever the latest gas price we have to pay, let's add another .25 cent fee per gallon of gas in America. America consumes 450 million gallons of gas a day. This means that if we invested those .25 cents per gallon, there would be 11.5 million dollars every day towards purchase of a Specific Purpose Bond called "SPB American Gas Bond". In only one month, the Bond would grow to 345 million and in a year, the Bond would be worth 4.14 billion dollars. Let's make America EXEMPT of our dependency on foreign oil. Let's us citizens invest 4.14 billion into American Gas Bonds that will focus on our own American oil, with emphasis for investment of alternate energies.

No longer would OPEC and others dictate and control how much we pay for a barrel of oil and a gallon of gas. Some of these oil countries that hate America are the very ones who fund terrorism, fly around in big jets, drive expensive luxury cars and live in palaces bathed in American profit money. While one particular country sells gas for $0.17 cents a gallon and wallows in their riches, America has been at their mercy hoping someday gas prices will be "cheaper."

Now that the Middle Eastern conglomerate has broken America's back in the oil industry, we are currently at their mercy when it comes to gas prices. How about we use the Specific Purpose American Gas Bond money to fund production of our OWN American oil wells and quickly become independent? How quickly you might ask? Imagine the power and authority we Americans would have being united together for a common cause such as this. Based on the above figures, how long do you think it would be before us Americans could afford to go into complete and full oil production at $40 dollars a barrel of oil and become totally independent of any other foreign entity? Hell, let's start buying out other oil companies here in America and set our own oil prices "for the American people and by the American people." By the way, if the plan is structured properly, the American Citizen bond holders, will vote to determine America's Oil prices and not Congress. The American Citizens will also be the only entity to vote money out of that Specific Purpose Bond and I reiterate once more, not Congress and not the President.

Many states in America have a lot of oil sitting in the ground that will cover our oil needs for the next 500 years. The problem is we can't compete with foreign oil prices, especially since they've started their conspiracy of selling a barrel of oil for less than $40 dollars per barrel, forcing American oil production to stop. Foreign nations were concerned that we might be able to offset some of our dependency by refining our own oil, so the Middle Eastern nations decided to break our bank of oil investors and caused America to close its oil wells. Well, they've almost succeeded. American oil investing, drilling and pumping is at an all-time low in America. Before American oil can be sold again, a profit has to be made by investors, which means we Americans can't start pumping any oil again until these foreign oil countries decide to raise the price of oil to $80 dollars or more per barrel. While the Middle East keeps their oil prices at or below $40 dollars per barrel, let's impose our own .25 cents per gallon Savings Bond immediately, while the prices for gas are still low. Who would have thought that owners of a small, desolate, sandy soil section of desert would one day control this great American nation of ours? Pathetic.

If America became independent of the necessity for oil, we citizens could easily bring the price of gas down to $1.50 per gallon again, and those profits would be returned to the "SPB American Gas Bond." The future gas prices could be controlled by a vote of the American Citizens (not Congress, not the President), for America. By the way, when you get a chance, go to the Web and take a look at the Natural Gas reserves we have. The reserves will astound you beyond your imagination. For those of you American Citizens who love the owls and hug the trees as I do, and would like to see that dirty, nasty oil just go away and become extinct, let's work together towards a logical common cause and solution. However, there is a fact we all need to ponder. A very small fraction of oil is used for those dirty filthy cars and trucks and the rest of that oil is used for making 6,000 other products like ladies nylons, pharmaceuticals, gun stocks, plastics of nearly every kind, cars, airplanes, toys, medicine bottles and bags and yada, yada, yada. Get it? Got it? Good.

Problem #2: Countries That Hate America. America has a long dark history of thinking money resolves the worlds' problems. Is a constant monetary handout ever appreciated, or a loan ever paid off? I believe America needs to deal with hostile countries as our first order of business. We Americans grew up in the knowledge of Love Thy Neighbor, but let's throw in a good dose of American Tough Love. I believe if any foreign nation is hateful towards Americans or citizens of the United States, they will not receive free monetary support of any kind as in the past. Any unwarranted aggression shown towards American Citizens, either residing or visiting in said foreign nations will be subject to a good dose of Tough Love. America has a history of helping all countries in need, especially during disasters and we should continue doing so. However, and to reiterate, those nations who support terrorism, kill American citizens, burn the American flag or espouse vulgarity or commit acts of aggression toward our country or our beliefs will receive no monetary support of any kind; not one scintilla.

A CLOSING THOUGHT: Well, now that we have stopped giving money away to hostile foreign countries, let's make good use of the money and invest those tens of millions in several more Special Purpose Bonds that can use the money to fund efforts needed here in America. As the money pot grows, keep in mind there are some Washington, D.C. foxes and chickens looking to get their sticky political fingers full of as much bond money as they can steal from the pot. At this point, it may be a good idea to ensure again that all of that saved money is directed towards a Specific Purpose Bond designated for a specific, finite purpose, instead of throwing it all in a big pile for criminal sticky fingers to grab. Think with me for a moment how many good things that Specific Purpose Bonds could accomplish? Other than the American Specific Purpose "SPB Gas Bond", another might be designated to help feed the poor, eliminate hunger in America or a bond to help house the needy, a National Disaster Specific Purpose Bond or a bond that offsets the cost of Healthcare. Again, the Specific Purpose Bonds, once designated, cannot be changed altered or used for any other purpose unless the American Citizenry votes its approval; not Congress and not the President. Our drained Social Security Fund is proof that sticky political fingered foxes and chickens just couldn't resist the temptation of helping themselves with our American money that was designated for a specific purpose, yet the thieving cowards in Congress figured out a way. Americans should be tired of being Congress's cash cow enablers by now.

A Hypothetical Example: Let's suppose America now has $342 billion dollars in the "SPB Fight Hunger in America". Each bond is indelibly marked for its specific purpose. The "SPB Fight Hunger in America" bond money is being used to offset those American citizens in need. As time passes, members of the D.C. sticky fingered group will probably be out looking to abscond with some of that Specific Purpose Bond money for another effort. In this hypothetical scenario, the sticky fingered group in Washington wants $43 million dollars to authorize themselves another 37% pay increase (as they have in the past). The only way Congress can get the money out of our "SPB Fight Hunger in America Specific Purpose Bond" account is to make their request known to the American Citizenry. American Citizens will vote

"Yes" or "No", and if we vote "No", that Specific Purpose Bond money better not be touched by anyone for any other purpose!

Then again, let's redirect the "SPB American Gas Bond" money towards going all solar or electric, or seek new sources of energy to drive cars other than using petroleum pollutants. I am positive that if we invested 11.5 million towards new energy solutions every day, it wouldn't take us Americans long to figure out what our priorities are and eliminate the dependency of sand people controlling our oil prices.

FACTOID: For six years, China was at the top of the list of foreign holders of U.S. Treasuries ($1.712 trillion), when it comes to loaning America money. Would someone please explain to me why we would borrow over a trillion dollars from China, and then our government turns right around and gives away $17.8 million of our tax dollars back to China for social and environmental programs for the Chinese people?

FACTOID: Japan is in second place as being at the top of the foreign holders of U.S. Treasuries ($1.197 trillion), when it comes to loaning America money. Would someone please explain to me why we would borrow that kind of money and then the U.S. Government would turn right around and spend $175,587.00 of our tax dollars to find out if cocaine makes Japanese quail engage in sexually risky behavior? Alas, this is a true statement. Putridity is personified by the greed at all levels of this American Nation of ours. What's the cure? You tell me......

josephusflaviussolo@gmail.com. I want to hear from you.

Chapter 3

———∾∾∾———

WEATHER ON THE ROCKS

FACT: Americans pay a lot of money to the U.S. National Weather Service (NWS.) The NWS is one of five other government agencies, and became a part of a higher tiered government agency called the National Oceanic and Atmospheric Administration (NOAA.)

CASE IN POINT: The National Weather Service (NWS), FY 2015 budget request asked for $1.06 billion dollars, a whopping $3.9 million above the 2014 enacted level. Our yearly cost for the 4,800 government workers is $750 million and with that an added $1.06 billion, NWS plans to upgrade their computer systems to be competitive with the more accurate, European Weather System.

DISCUSSION: The National Weather Service has 121 Field Offices, 13 River Forecast Centers, 9 National Centers and with that $4.5 billion modernization program money, the NWS wants a 12 minute tornado lead time instead of a 6 minute lead time. Now that is quite an improvement over what the government did from 1937 to 1952.

Unbelievably, and during those years, the government weather service did not share any of their tornado knowledge because they didn't want to "incite panic." However in 1938 the government weather service did give tornado warnings to emergency management personnel only. Then, in 1952, us common typical average American Citizens were finally told about impending tornado threats. In 1870, the Weather Bureau was established through a joint resolution of Congress. The military ran the program until the civilian government took it over in 1890. Citizens, we OWN the American system of government. Let's begin to make logical decisions and think more innovatively.

J. SOLO'S SOLUTION: All lives are precious. The loss of one American life because of adverse weather is one too many. However, it is a fact that the European Weather Service has continuously reported American weather more accurately than our National Weather Service ever has. That is, until the U.S. Government spends another $25 billion to upgrade NWS computers! Why do we need to spend so much money for a computer system, when a far more accurate weather system has already been in place for years in Europe? Several instances have already occurred where European weather data for hurricanes and tornados did not agree with NWS weather here in America, and the European weather was correct and far more accurate every time.

Here's the deal. Let's subcontract the far more accurate European Weather Service and eliminate the National Weather Service. Vector all the money saved to a Special Purpose Bond that ends world hunger. For local weather, go out in your yard and hang a rock on a string where you can see it from your favorite window. If the rock is wet, it's raining. If it has white stuff on it, I predict either frost or snow would be a good guess, and if that rock is swinging it's probably going to be windy out there. That rock will even tell you the intensity of an earthquake by jumping up and down on its string! In the meantime, we can get our accurate weather from our European neighbors, who know how to accurately forecast and predict weather, while saving billions of dollars, without the National Weather Service organization.

A CLOSING THOUGHT: Using a rock, and subcontracting the European Weather Service will save Americans over $1 billion a year – let's take that money and buy a $1 billion dollar Specific Purpose Bond for something good every year!

FACTOID: An average of 610 Americans die each year due to weather related issues.

josephusflaviussolo@gmail.com

Chapter 4

———∿∿∿———

DESTINATION SPACE: WHO VOTED FOR THAT ONE?

FACT: Trillions of American dollars are being spent on the space program. The military industrial complex gets over 600 billion each year.

DISCUSSION: Since the United States entered the space program in the 1960's, billions of U.S. dollars were used to "beat" Russia to the moon. Well, I guess we did, but I fail to understand what mattered after we got there. Moon rocks were brought back, goofy expensive moon cars were developed for the astronauts to drive around in the dirt and sing along as they merrily rolled over the moon's surface, and then we planted a flag. Big deal. Somehow, we've lost interest in the earth and its inhabitants and we're ready to explore new frontiers in the farther reaches of space. After countless years of scanning the skies every night, using deep space observation techniques, I fail to recognize the value added. The conquest to Mars seems to be the next focus in our endeavor to exist on a planet that is absolutely hostile to earthlings.

Somehow, all that money we are spending will finally convince the planet of Mars to settle down and become friendly, just by osmosis alone. In the interim, we have a new recent discovery of a planet that is fully capable of some form of life as we know it. This planet is 63 trillion light years away and by golly, we just need to throw some more money at it until we find out more about whether or not we are alone in the cosmos. I would not doubt there is presently a project underway that will speed a module into the heavens and land on that planet. Oh, by the way, it will take that particular "module" 63 trillion years to land after traveling at the speed of light, which is 186,000 miles per second. Suffice it to say that you and I won't be here to watch that momentous occasion. The U.S. spent $25 billion dollars to get man on the moon. NASA's Shuttle Program cost $209 billion alone. We have made 51 attempts to send a spacecraft to Mars and what for? I simply don't remember voting for this expense. I am fully aware that we Americans have a budget every year, and our government has representatives on our behalf, working to provide for our needs, but somewhere along the way, the budget just continues morphing and forking over tons and tons of money to continue space exploration when we haven't figured out all there is to know about our own planet or its oceans! When was the last time your representatives in congress asked you about what other projects we could spend trillions of dollars on? Hopefully, something other than a Space Program, that after 50 years we have nothing to show but a bunch of really cool pictures of outer space, and proved the moon is dirt and now there is an apparent urgency to get to Mars.

CASE IN POINT: Is there a new conspiracy out there I may not be aware of? Why have we spent 50 years trying to get off this planet? Can't we just be thankful for what we have and leave space alone for a while, and let all of the space debris presently orbiting this earth fall to the ground before we clutter it up with more junk? It is a fact that there is a privately funded civilian space program that does have a mission to get to Mars. In the meantime, NASA thinks they need to compete against the private American company and are throwing even more money away trying to get there before they do. NASA used to be in the business of beating Russia to the Moon. Now NASA wants to compete against a private space company right here in America. Somebody tell them we're on the same side for heaven's sake!

J. SOLO'S SOLUTION: I believe we do need to continue space exploration for military defense programs. I also believe there should be a focus to spend more of our money towards medical research and technology. However, money being spent for American citizens to live on the Moon or Mars, or any other planet is ludicrous and a complete waste. All government funded space programs should be required to submit a Project Plan that includes just exactly what the mission is comprised of and intends to accomplish. Visiting Mars or the Moon are not projects that would create any value added unless extreme necessity is relevant. We need to focus more on this planet and spend money on other programs dedicated towards other concerns, like a cure for cancer, heart disease, diabetes or deal with the problems of American poverty and education just to name a few more important subjects we are faced with every day, right here on our own marble, and leave the other marbles out there in space alone. If there is another life form out there somewhere my hands are not going to be outstretched asking, "what are you going to give me" when and if they land here on earth. Besides, how do we know "they" are friendly? Who knows that some evil alien force has been listening to us for the last 60 years, to our frenzied constant flow of radio data we've been transmitting throughout the cosmos? Us humans could be looked upon by an evil alien force as "their" food source, and become "their" cattle supply. Don't we already have enough problems? It might be a good time to start losing a little weight though. Who would have known that humans had become the alien's first choice on the menu and those evil aliens have found a delicacy in the taste of human fat in their diet? Now I even have more incentive to begin losing a few pounds.

Stop the extravagant money spent on Mars and save those billions of dollars for a Specific Purpose Bond. And, let's title that Specific Purpose Bond, "STOP CRIME IN AMERICA." How many American Citizens do you know who would oppose stopping crime? Yet, we are quick to fund money to live on the moon and mars. I can hear the Artificial Intelligence (AI), on the overhead intercom, "Ladies and them! We welcome you all aboard our new gravity free space vehicle, the ASs1! Our Dinkydo Hyperspeed promises arrival in one hour. Mars is only a warm congenial 345 degrees today, so sit back and hydrate yourself as much as you can, with plenty of our complimentary non alcohol beverage "Mint Julipious." As a reminder, please let any member of our staff know if your Julipious tastes a little salty or smells like frog water. Unfortunately, we have been having difficulties with our conversion unit, filtering your pee pee into fresh water. So, enjoy, and have a great day from all of us morons aboard ASs1." Most of all, please remember our famous motto, "Where else can you get a free drink and a good pee."

FACTOID: Did you know NASA continues to spend 1 million dollars a year developing "a Mars menu", just in case they figure out a way to waste and consume more billions and billions of dollars to put a man on a hostile planet?

FACTOID: Scientists know there are at least 100 billion galaxies out there, that some may be a friendly habitat for earthlings. That's why we're spending billions for telescopes, new rocketry and space food and doing everything we can to find a replacement earth. Scientists know our Sun is 1/3rd through its lifetime and when it gets to ½ of its lifetime, the sun's brightness intensity will get even warmer and begin to dry up our humidity and dry up our oceans. So, is that why Americans in the science world are hastily looking for a new home somewhere in space? I have no idea why NASA wants us to live on Mars, knowing our only hope will be an exoplanet. In February of 2016, scientists estimated there were 700 quintillion terrestrial exoplanets. These units are planets that do not revolve around our sun. But, rather, other suns in the galaxy out in the far reaches of space. I find it interesting that scientists are absolutely sure our earth is doomed and we need to look elsewhere because our earth will be no more.......... in about 200 billion more years – well, who the hell cares!

In the meantime, the money pours in so we can look way out into the vast reaches of space. Sounds like a con job for Job Security to me, right scientists?

Although I am personally a stargazer, I have no interest in moving to Mars, nor do I feel my tax dollars should fund such nonsense. If NASA or Space X wants to explore extra-terrestrial frontiers, I suggest a Special Purpose Bond, "SPB Moon/Mars" bond be created, and all of those interested Americans can purchase specific bonds that will support and fund future space exploration. I am not a proponent for purchase of this bond, but I am sure there are numerous interested Americans that have no problem whatsoever in making an investment towards that cause. Just leave me and my tax money out of the Moon/Mars effort. For those who have invested in the Moon/Mars bond, I wish you well as you all fly off to a hostile planet. This earth-bound hostile planet is enough for me.

josephusflaviussolo@gmail.com

Fact: The International Space Station is represented by 15 nations. Some of those 15 nations are hostile towards America. The ISS remains in low orbit and travels a speed of 25 times our commercial aircraft and 9 times faster than a speeding bullet. It can circle the earth every 92 or so minutes. Annual costs to fly the ISS are 3 billion dollars. Since 1998, we have spent 75 billion dollars and the ISS will complete its mission in 2024, while total costs are expected to reach 100 to 162 billion dollars. How nice. The question might be "who" of the 15 nations has contributed the most money towards this effort? Of the 15 nations, "we" are the ones funding most of the bill. For what? What is the value added for such a cost and what has its existence in space done towards medicine, health, crime, starvation and peace with security on this earth? Where is our demand for a Specific Purpose Bond that addresses problems right here on the grounds of the U.S.A.? Somehow our government representatives are the ones who are "elected" to decide how we spend our tax money. They sure as hell don't represent me. I'm looking for a Specific Purpose Bond that addresses the issue of things like people who have to go to bed hungry each night, or an SPB that eradicates crime or war. When congress stands out on the front line of hunger, crime and war with a Specific Purpose Bond I will be right behind them, because then I will know those elected representatives of the government are doing positive things for the betterment of this country and its citizens. Isn't that what you elite pontificating group of unintelligent asses are supposed to do up there in Washington, D.C.? The intent of government representation was established in the Constitution, "for the people and by the people." Sadly, more and more people are beginning to research our American history and are learning that most of our representatives are not listening or learning the message of our documented American historical failures. Those representatives who represent us are more focused upon their own desires of venality before they think about you and I. Should anyone disagree, consider following the money trail first to see where the downward spiral takes you.

josephusflaviussolo@gmail.com

Chapter 5

———∿∿∿———

All that Energy of
Poo Poo Power

FACT: Human waste will continue to be a perpetual commodity until someone figures out how we can go poopless. Most countries dump their raw sewage in the oceans, while others have disposal treatment plants.

DISCUSSION: China has been using its raw sewage as fertilizer for centuries, as has Japan. However, by not maximizing its potential first, the discarded sewage has attributed to an unhealthy environment to propagate germ and disease, including pollution of our oceans. Some countries have become quite innovative in the treatment of its sewage. Incorporating alternate methods involving more effective treatment plants and fabrication of specialized toilets capable of processing germ free human waste that can be safely used to fertilize, makes logic sense. Many countries are beginning to realize the importance and advantages of recycling human waste. Unfortunately, there have been no large scale attempts to maximize its potential.

CASE IN POINT: England came up with a 40-seat bus that runs on methane gas. On a full tank of methane, it can average 186 miles. This bus is running on a Poo Poo product. Methane CH4, is 20 times more potent than CO2. It is invisible, odorless and present in trace concentrations in the atmosphere. Methane is the major component of natural gas, being 87% to 96%. Methanogens are our largest source of methane producing bacteria found in swamps and wetlands. Methane has an explosive nature that can be confirmed by most teenagers who have put a match to their butthole units. Methane gas is everywhere, so poop, let's do something with it besides lighting fires.

J. SOLO'S SOLUTION: Years ago my daughter and I were out riding horses, and as many equestrians, cowboys and Indians know, it is "not a good thing to let your horse eat a lot of green grass when out on the trail." Well, my daughter wouldn't pull up on the reins to prevent ingestion of that greenery because she felt sorry for the poor horse and let him eat freely as we plodded down the trail. It wasn't long before her horse began digesting the grass and farting like a chicken! Unfortunately, my daughter was in the lead and I was following and I thought someone had gassed the area with a nauseous sulfur bomb! Needless to say, that old horse has been fondly remembered as "Old Fart Bag" over the years. Old Fart Bag and methane gas gave me an idea. Congestive Obstructive Pulmonary Disease (COPD), patients are using breathing devices such as oxygen-enriched tanks or portable oxygen generators that draw in regular air and filters out the hydrogen, leaving an oxygen rich environment. These portable oxygen generators gave me the thought that each home could have a Methane Generator, using the same concept as a portable oxygen generator, capable of extracting higher rates of methane. The Methane Generator would come supplied with a 5/8's inch hose and a 4" screw cap that would screw on a sewer cleanout and sniff out every bit of methane gas floating around right down your very own sewer line and beyond. The Methane Generator would immediately begin extracting methane gas and storing it in a tank that would supply all of your home heating, hot water and cooking needs. So, the initial cost of your Methane Generator would be a one-time event (with insurance) and could supply each household with nearly a free source of energy for many years. Well, poop, how easy was that problem to solve?

josephusflaviussolo@gmail.com

FACT: The following story is not true, but has humor.

Japan was having a serious sewage problem in the ocean off Tokyo. That was where tons and tons of raw sewage and mud gathered along its coast. So, they turned to a scientist, asking him what could be done with the sewage. Mitsuyuki Ikedacon came up with a process of blending the raw sewage with soya and "the red substance, when fried, looks and tastes just like beef!" Now I know exactly why I stopped eating beef in 1973. However, this is sensational news for those of you who can't stand some of your relatives you have to put up with as I have over the years. Hence, The Shit Burger! Simply drop your aggression, take a deep breath and chill out. In fact, let bygones be bygones, and invite all your mean relatives over for a tasty Shit Burger Barbeque! Got a nagging mother-in-law, a pompous nosey neighbor you can't stand or a sesquipedalian sister-in-law that never shuts up and looks like someone beat her face with a bag of nickels? Well, here's your chance to have some fun, man, it's stink'in payback time! For the loquacious big mouth at the barbeque or the boss you never liked, fix him up a Double Shit Burger! Here's the best part. After they've eaten the burgers and seem happy, explain to them how Eco friendly the Shit Burgers are and how much money you've saved not having to buy expensive beef products. I guarantee that will be the last time you ever hear from them again! The scientist says the current price for the burger is 10 to 20 times the regular beef price and is loaded with up to 63% protein. But wait until the fast food chains get wind of this, (pun intended!)

Once they figure out the mass production savings, they'll be selling this crap to everybody until the U.S. Government intervenes with a better fail program. I'm thinking politicians will figure out a way to make money by feeding these tasty little shit burgers to all of the prisoners in America. After parole, I'm convinced these people will never, ever want to go to prison again, or ever vote for a politician again. Now that America has eliminated Japan's problems, we can begin taking more shit off of all of the other countries like we already have over the years. Better yet, let's expand this thought and develop something nutritious for the vegetarians or those who are looking to acquire even more fiber and grains in their diet. How about the classic Cow Turd Burger? We can mass produce the Japan made processor, and begin producing cow shit and soya burgers. One can only imagine the attributes of a healthy, high fiber diet for the criminal politicians in D.C.

If you think this is a crazy idea in a world gone mad, someone needs to tell me why you can purchase a very costly coffee made out of cat shit. Yet, another subject you might want to surf the Web to validate. It really is an available product, and much sought after by those who appreciate a finer blend of coffee. Oh my...."Bucket List"

FACTOID: Did you know our government gave $168,766 dollars of our tax money to study monkeys throwing monkey poop? Now, that right there is an obvious waste of money. Who in their right mind could think of spending money like that on monkeys? Why didn't the government spend the money for a study of a wild pack of poop throwing orangutans? They can throw poop twice as far! Boy, I hope we get to use those orangutans when congress is in session for "the real live shit fest!" It could be the next TV hit Series! I'll bet some of the attendees at the congress shit fest might even be related to one another! Then Pelosi came to mind. OK, I apologize to my fellow senior citizens ahead of time for that one. Senior citizens like her really are a good lot of people and should know when it's time to retire. Greet the senior ones around you when and while you can because their journey has a close ending and a new beginning in eternity at a far away place. Choose your destiny wisely.

FACTOID: Why do we call them congressmen anyway? If "pro" means for and "con" means against, why are we calling these people "con"gressmen? If they are doing nothing for the American Citizens, they must be "cons". If they really are cons, why don't we clean up the mess and call them Progressmen and Progresswomen? Then, let's make sure their purpose is for Progress, instead of a "con"gress job.

josephusflaviussolo@gmail.com

Chapter 6

NUCLEAR STUFF #1

FACTOID: Since 1960, the U.S. began using nuclear power reactors as a source of energy. Of course, generating nuclear power has had its hazards just as we have had by using alternate sources such as oil and coal powered units. However nuclear reactors create a ton of waste and America isn't sure what to do with it.

DISCUSSION: In 2014, the 100 reactors we have in America, produced 798 billion kilowatt hours (kWh), and another five reactors were under construction. In 2002, the Bush Administration approved of the Yucca Mountain Project in Nevada to store 70,000 tons of radioactive nuclear waste in a series of tunnels 600 feet below the surface of the ground. After the government appropriated $9 billion dollars for construction of the Yucca Mountain Project, the Obama Administration came along in 2010 and cut nearly all funding due to the war effort in the Middle East. In the meantime, some scientists proposed we pack our nuclear waste up in rockets and shoot the waste into outer space. Others said we should use it as an alternate energy resource and recycle the waste.

CASE IN POINT: The idea of sending 70,000 tons of nuclear waste into deep space is crazy. Do some of these high salary scientists and congressmen ever have to take a logic test or a brain scan? Even if we sent 5 pounds of nuclear waste at a time it would take 28 million rockets to send our waste into deep space. If only one of those 28 million rockets fail, we could expect a radiation cloud and an aluminum dust debris field in the atmosphere that would kill millions of people, (of course the government wouldn't hesitate in wasting our tax money to finance the 28 million rockets, right?) The suggestion to recycle nuclear waste on planet earth was banned in the U.S., fearing it could be used for nuclear weapons. I can't see how our recycling of nuclear waste can lead to being used as a nuclear weapon unless we assign a big fox to watch the hen house. Then to make matters worse, in 2015, Nevada was given three new national monuments, thanks to our plethora of mindless members in Congress. And wouldn't you know it, the Basin and Range National Monument just happened to be the very same 704,000 acres of land right above where we spent 9 billion dollars of good tax money to store our nuclear waste 600 feet below! Apparently the fox IS watching the hen house because it didn't take the Yucca Mountain Project program managers long to realize they now have a major problem. So, the main tunnel and railroad tracks already in place beneath the surface that are going to be used to store all of that nuclear waste now just happens to be directly beneath the 704,000 acre National Monument! Can this get any worse? Yes, only in America can we screw things up so eloquently. The Yucca Mountain Project proposed funding to accommodate 70,000 tons of waste, but now we have 75,000 tons of waste. By the way, I might add at this juncture that some of this waste will remain radioactive for the next 210,000 years. As of this writing, spent nuclear waste is stored in a combination of pools, dry casks, stored in tanks or in concrete or steel bunkers in close proximity of all of our nuclear reactors in America, whether they are producing or not. In 1977, America banned any and all programs to recycle the waste for fear that some bad guys might get ahold of it and make a nuclear weapon, in spite of the fact that foreign nations are already recycling their own nuclear waste. For now the only logical program worth considering at this point is to recycle our nuclear waste. So, while the brilliance of our congress and executive branch is preoccupied in chasing the fearsome global warming trends, declaring a National Monument of 704,000 acres right over the top of an intended nuclear waste storage area is the epitome of complete stupidity. Congress gets more of nothing done for America while prancing around most of our critical problems. Dear Americans; we have 75,000 tons (150 million pounds) of nuclear waste that's just full of radiation lying around waiting for a train that can't roll down the tracks to the underground storage facilities because there is a big national monument up above. Until this host of congressional empty suits and dysfunctional administration begins to act, we are at an impasse. Gosh, maybe those congress people could pass out speeding tickets at the Indy 500?

FACTOID: We need to at least commend our U.S. Senators. Their hair has been looking great for the last 30 years by spending 5.25 million of our taxpaying dollars looking dapper for the dam damsels and the remaining fossils who continue to shuffle through the D.C. hallways.

J. SOLO'S SOLUTION: There may be a workable solution to this problem as you read on in the next topic of discussion titled Nuclear Stuff #2. Hang with me and read on because this topic is getting exciting – almost nuclear and "nuculer" as George W. might say.

josephusflaviussolo@gmail.com

Chapter 7

NUCLEAR STUFF #2

FACT: Since the 1950's, we have been using nuclear generators to provide a near free electrical energy source that has the potential of producing electrical energy for 1,000 years in duration. There is one generator that has only one moving part that needs replacement every 14 to 17 years.

DISCUSSION: Did you know Radioisotope Thermoelectric Generators (RTG or RITEG), have been in use for the last 60+ years? The NASA space programs have been using them. They have been one of the primary sources of electrical supply for nearly all remote missions in space, where the Sun cannot provide enough solar energy to support the electrical energy load. The RTG has no moving parts to wear out and needs no routine maintenance program. They are supplied by low-grade radioactive nuclear energy, (I would like to interject at this juncture that it doesn't take a brilliant mind to immediately think of what we might be able to do with "low-grade nuclear energy", especially after having read that we have 75,000 tons if it laying around America without a home or a purpose.)

CASE IN POINT: Some Russian owned lighthouses near the Arctic Circle have been using low-grade nuclear waste energy to generate electricity for many, many decades. Our remote ocean beacons have been powered by Radioisotope Thermoelectric Generators for a very long time. RTG's were one of the most useful sources of nuclear/electric energy in 1966 by the U.S. Navy at Fairway Rock in Alaska until 1995. The RTG's were powered by decaying plutonium 238. Since 1961, the NASA space programs have used RTG's for 28 space missions like Pioneer, Voyager, Galileo, Ulysses, New Horizons, the Apollo Missions and the Mars Science Laboratory, just to name a few. Well, as time passed some innovative minds got together and came up with a more efficient dynamic generator that can provide 4 times the conversion energy of the old RTG's. The next-generation radioisotope-fueled power source called the Advanced Stirling Radioisotope Generator (ASRG), uses one moving part, which is a piston on each end that is surrounded by nitrogen gas that reduces wear and this unit will run for 17 continuous years. A small ASRG can produce 130 watts of power using only 2 pounds of plutonium for 17 years. So, let's make a great big ASRG that uses 2,000 pounds of highly radioactive waste. Now, we have a generator that will provide 130,000 watts continually for 17 years producing enough free energy for 83,200 homes. Does plutonium wear out? Yes, Plutonium-239 has a half-life of 24,400 years. That means the only thing that will wear out is the ASRG engine after 17 years. So, 2,000 pounds of nuclear waste will produce 130,000 watts (130 Mega Watts), of power during the next 24,400 years. While the prices for coal, oil, solar and other petroleum products cost more and more each year, the Space Administration has had exclusive rights and use of these ASRG's for long-term exploration and science missions into deep, deep space and even to Mars and other planets!

I guess we don't have a need or use for any kind of generator that uses low-grade radioactive waste energy that would create a cost saving source of electrical energy here on Earth for generations to come. Now is the time for us to think about that 75,000 tons of nuclear radioactive "waste" that is still waiting for the train stopped dead in its tracks because of politics. The remaining nuclear reactors that power American homes that are presently using nuclear energy will produce another 500 pounds of highly radioactive waste each year that we STILL can't bury 600 feet deep beneath a National Monument.

J. SOLO'S SOLUTION: I hope by now you have been following my reasoning for all of the information you have read in Nuclear Stuff #1 and #2. We have learned there are 75,000 tons (that's 150 million pounds), of radioactive waste that will lay around with a half-life of 24,000 thousand years. Heck, I am so worked up at this point, I'm not even going to elaborate on another nuclear waste product called Uranium-235 that has a half-life of 710,000 years! Here are a few facts we know. One is that since 1977, America signed a law that none of that nuclear waste can be used for anything because bad guys might make bombs out of it, right? Well, if the bad guys wanted nuclear waste, why don't they go and round up all of the ocean beacon lights Russia has been using for the last 60 years or raid a remote lighthouse and steal its nuclear waste? Another fact is that European and other foreign nations are already using their nuclear waste. Are you beginning to understand the reasoning here? Here I go again with yet another idea that continues to smack of logic. While I do not profess to be a nuclear physicist or scientist it just seems logical to me that we could run a series of Advanced Stirling Radioisotope Generators right next to that train loaded with nuclear waste stalled on the tracks, waiting for the government to authorize safe storage for the 600 foot descent down into the tunnels. I would not be surprised that those Advanced Stirling Radioisotope Generators could easily provide all of Americas' supply of electrical energy for generations to come. Oh, and JUST ABOUT COST FREE!

No. Not really free. If ASRG's were placed on line producing America's needs, we could freeze the current cost for energy at the present prices we are paying each month, and utilize the offset profits to invest in some more Specific Purpose Bonds. Imagine how quickly America could pay off our National Debt of 30 something + trillion dollars. There are a plethora of Bonds we could create that would never incur debt. With this plan, like all other proposals, it would save money to purchase Specific Purpose Bonds and American Citizens would have exclusive rights to vote on the authorization of any changes once a Specific Purpose Bond is established. I am honestly beginning to think donation of the 704,000 acres for a national monument above the nuclear underground storage site was politically done on purpose. I also feel that we Americans have had the capability to produce near free electrical energy and it has been known for years. Why else would America rush to prohibit use of nuclear waste back in 1977, supposedly afraid the boogey man might make bombs out of the waste? If that's the case America has nuclear waste scattered all over our nuclear facilities and continues to have nuclear waste "temporarily" stored all over this country for the last 60 years, and I have not heard of any boogey men helping themselves to it yet. Besides, Iran is blossoming with nuclear stuff as you read this book. Let's just hope it's for electrical energy and not stupidity. What do you suppose they might do with their nuclear waste?

josephusflaviussolo@gmail.com

FACTOID: The National Science Foundation spent $216 thousand dollars to study whether or not American politicians "gain or lose support by taking ambiguous positions." Are we in trouble here in America or what?

FACTOID: Most car engines weigh about 350 pounds. A quick research of the new Omega 1 engine will reveal an engine that weighs 38 pounds and is capable of producing 160 horsepower. Each engine can be stacked to increase horsepower. Two engines weighing 76 pounds are capable of producing 320 horsepower. The engine can run on various fuels and hydrogen, so let's take a look at our options before we run American cars on the current electrical grid system. By the way, the current American electrical grid system is dependent upon fossil fuels to generate electrical energy. The more electrical demand we create, the more fossil fuel it will take to run all of our electric cars. My electric car is fantastic and it does not pollute the air as much as other cars and trucks do. For those driving the all electric cars and trucks, 500 miles is made possible only because it required fossil fuels to power the electrical grids. On average, it takes about 84 pounds of coal or 6 barrels of oil to charge an electric car. California has nearly 18 million cars on the road each day. If all cars were electric, it would take one billion, five hundred and twelve million (1,512,000,000) pounds of coal, or four billion, three hundred and twenty million gallons (4,320,000,000) of oil each time the 18 million cars are charged. One can only imagine how many more fossil pollutants will fill the air. It seems that nuclear energy has become a pariah instead of a blessing. Yes. Nuclear can be used to destroy and kill all of mankind. Well, so can a biological germ agent. When are we going to look at the positive aspects of an energy free society and realize the usefulness of nuclear energy to use for the good of the people? Instead, politicians remind us of the ever-present dark fear of a nuclear threat that can destroy all of mankind in a nuclear war and nuclear threat is so terrifying and horrible, earthlings have become afraid to make it useful and nearly cost free. Knives are deadly if used for evil, baseball bats are deadly if used for evil, driving a car can be deadly if used for evil. However, the value added by safely using large quantities of nuclear waste could be a genius plan. Otherwise, the nuclear waste is just going to sit at locations all over the United States and do nothing but radiate instead of providing pollution free energy for millennia, (and yes, I am aware there are companies presently using small quantities of nuclear waste, but the bad part is that someday, we all will be paying some giant nuclear company that uses the ASRG engine. By then, it will be too late for us to consider that if we had a Special Purpose Bond program for funding the use of nuclear waste, our electrical bill would be free for thousands of years. We, (America's Citizens), are the ones that should own our energy (politicians would have a hissy fit if all citizens OWNED free energy, because we paid for it and we want our energy free, or at least nearly free.

FACTOID: I find it interesting that the Stirling Engine was patented in 1918. Instead of humanity being preoccupied to make weapons of war and killing people with nuclear energy, America could have been using the good benefits of nuclear power and free electrical energy could have been possible many decades ago. Politics, greed and power has suppressed free energy technology via safe nuclear radioisotope energy, while politics taught us to fear its destructive power. How long has it been since we had to hide beneath our school desks and close our eyes to the lies we were told? For years, school children, shaking in fear, with closed eyes and hiding (and some crying) under their chairs, waiting for the blast. What a line of crap. You got us real scared – but for how much longer do you suppose we'll continue to be scared, before logic arrives in the minds of a plethora of thinkers? I can only wonder.

Socrates stated "Wisdom begins in wonder." I find it biblically captivating the Bible states "The Fear of the Lord is the Beginning of Wisdom." Does human wisdom reign on this planet?

josephusflaviussolo@gmail.com

Chapter 8

THE PERPETUAL ENERGY GLOBE

How many of us remember the Crookes Radiometer as seen in this photo?

Discussion: My science teacher had one of these small novelty units and it was always fun watching the spinning black and white flags at the top while longing to get back to dissecting one of those nasty old dead frogs again. Each flag or vane is painted white on one side and black on the other side. When placed near sunlight the sun the flags would spin like crazy. This little unit would also spin if you put it in a refrigerator because the black panels absorb the cold and start turning again. Sir William Crookes invented the device, but the scientific explanation for the rotation was not even known until 1879. The radiometer consists of a glass bulb in a partial vacuum with a set of vanes mounted at the top of a tiny pointed spindle. The flags or vanes, rotate when exposed to light, which goes even faster as the light intensity increases. I suppose science classes are showing students the Crookes Radiometer even today. This little heat and cold engine has no moving parts to wear out and is powered by free energy from the sun or the cold of night.

CASE IN POINT: I've been watching my old Crookes Radiometer for 40 years and still am amazed at how this device never needs a battery. As long as there is a source of light from a nearby light bulb or sunlight, this little unit will be waving its flags at me just spinning along as freely as can be. So many times I wondered if I put this unit outside, would it spin forever in the sun's light and continue spinning even when it gets cold?

J. SOLO'S SOLUTION: Is this close to perpetual energy and is there a way to tap into this source to provide free energy? Maybe:

We already know this device works, but because it is small, I'm thinking it probably doesn't have very much torque (driving force), so if the spindle turned and we attached a series of graduating gears at the bottom, could it turn a generator of some kind? If so, let's find us a desert property out there in the wilderness of the state somewhere and build a small working replica of the little Crookes Radiometer. At the base of the spindle attach a gearing mechanism that, through a series of step-up or step-down gears, it could drive a generator that would produce a near perpetually free source of electrical energy. Presently, we are using this technology with wind turbines and wind vanes, why not build a Crookes Radiometer the size of three football fields? You probably remember the story in Nuclear Stuff #1 where 704,000 acres was mistakenly (or purposefully), dedicated by the government as the Basin and Range National Monument right over the top of the intended nuclear storage tunnels? It would make sense to rescind that as a National Monument and by doing so, allow the train to tunnel down into the 600 foot storage caverns with the 75,000 tons of radioactive waste and now we have all of that 704,000 acres on the surface to place several giant Crookes Radiometers! While the Advanced Stirling Radioisotope Generators (ASRG's) are generating tons of Gigawatts of electricity from the nuclear waste stored in the tunnels, the large Crookes Radiometers above ground are supplementing yet another FREE alternate source of electricity.

josephusflaviussolo@gmail.com

Chapter 9

—∽∼∾—

THE CO-OP FREE ENERGY CITY

FACT: Each city in America is supplied electrical energy sources from a few very large electrical generating plants here in America using combinations of natural gas, wind power, coal, water turning generators or nuclear power plants. Unfortunately, coal and nuclear power is becoming more unpopular, citing a plethora of reasons for or against. More and more, we are beginning to look at new and innovative means of creating energy that doesn't adversely impact or impair the beauty of an American environment.

DISCUSSION: I am a strong proponent of using all the resources available to provide this country with the cleanest air we can achieve. It seems that before we can entice other states, cities and nations to follow, we're going to need to lead by example. How about we select an average city and modify it to become a Free Energy Model City that does not use sources from an electrical grid or natural gas? Before we let Congress go in to a monetary hog-wild production let's select a small average city like Manteca, California and introduce the "SPB Manteca

Bond" program. Congress could invest on behalf of the American citizens and shower grant money all over the Manteca Bond, instead of being so senseless and throwing away good money for Quail and Monkey research. Once the city of Manteca is modified and changed into a positive working example of an energy free city, it would serve as the motivating force and encourage other cities to do the same. It would certainly demonstrate to other countries and boast of our success. (and congress can be proud of something for once.)

CASE IN POINT: If we expect the world to follow our lead in clean air then we really need to demonstrate a viable, working model.

J. SOLO'S SOLUTION: Construct a model Co-Op Free Energy City. The U.S. Government should announce its support towards enabling and assisting an American city that would like to be a candidate to become Co-OP. In this example, let's use a typically small town population of 75,000 like Manteca, California. Funded by Government Grant money and SPB Manteca Bonds (Special Prupose Bonds purchased by American citizens), construct an energy efficient pole that will replace every light pole within the city limits of Manteca. Each energy efficient light pole would incorporate multiple sides equipped with solar cells. Near its top, are two or more wind generator vanes and at the top of every pole is a Crookes Radiometer. Methane gas can easily be extracted and stored at each home for heating and cooking needs. Taking the aforementioned energy resources into consideration regarding the total output requirements to run the city of Manteca, one engineer could be contracted by the city manager or mayor to determine the additional energy needs for the city and wind generators and solar collectors could be installed as necessary. All homes in Manteca will have the maximum number of solar panels installed and all windows except safety glass, will be replaced with transparent solar windows. Nearly all cattle grazing and croplands could have transparent solar panels that would not detrimentally affect the normal plant growth in the fields or diminish crop production. Giant Radiometer domes could be constructed using transparent or tinted plastic solar cells, and the entire dome inside area could be used for agriculture, a giant Eco park, farmland or even tons of homes for the needy under the protection of the dome. The intent here is to enable the city of Manteca to provide its own electrical needs and get off the main power plant grids. In fact, Manteca could easily produce excess energy that could be sold back to the grid. If solar, wind and Methane resources are not enough, use some of that 75 thousand tons of radioactive waste that's scattered all over America.

Who pays for all of this? American citizens who invest in this bond and a few grants from Uncle Sam. After the city of Manteca becomes energy efficient, we can proudly boast about the "The Co-Op Free Energy City" and show it as an example to other cities all across America. Of course, there will be a continued need for maintenance and workers, but at some point the residents of Manteca could or should be paying less for its energy. Monetary savings by having an energy free city would pay the total cost of the effort in no time at all. As time passes, many other cities would see Manteca as an example of success, and have the desire to become a Co-Op Free Energy City as well. Future cities who want to do what Manteca has done will be able to request funding for their city from the Special Purpose Bond (SPB Energy Free City).

A CLOSING THOUGHT: It all sounds easy. It is not. One thing in our favor is that every bit of technology that would be needed is currently available, and we have all the resources to make this energy-free city possible. We are presently using major electric power grids here in America, that if to an enemy decided to take them out, it would be a long time before we turned on a light or had a gallon of gas to pump into our gas tank. Every convenience we know of depends on electricity. Take those few major power plant grids out and we'll all be riding horses again for four to ten years before we recover. The other point

I want to make here is we would continue to dig for coal and natural gas. The only difference is that instead of having to use it, we can sell it to the other nations. If the bad guys ever came for the major power plant grids, there would be a number of surviving cities still providing their own energy. In terms of value added; by taking on this monetary venture and the expense it would incur that might otherwise, dissuade your support of this endeavor, let's reason together by taking a look at the 4 Trillion dollars that we spent fighting Al Qaeda in the Middle East with the realization of having nothing to show for it but dead soldiers and courageous disabled veterans. Another example would be the 25 billion dollars we wasted to drive a silly car or walk on Moon dirt and plant a flag and place retro-reflectors so that one day we could shoot a laser beam at a point on the moon and the reflective light will return to earth – whoop dee doo, who cares! While I am not opposed to spending money, I believe the words "value added" should be a primary consideration other than beating Russia to the moon. By the way, I hear the city of Manteca is now investing its profit money in a Specific Purpose Bond called "The Free Energy Co-Op City." It would probably be a good investment if it were true. If it was a true story, and you are an American citizen, you would qualify to purchase these specific purpose bonds as well – not China and not Japan or any other foreign nation and become a profit sharing holder of these bonds.

FACTOID: Instead of spending our taxpayers money on grants for value added projects, here are a few oxymorons the morons in the government would rather spend our tax money on: A $325 thousand dollar grant to develop a "Robosquirrel". Yes folks, a robotic rodent designed to test the interaction between rattlesnakes and squirrels. Great! Now, there's going to be a bunch of robotic squirrels bumping into the House and Senate politicians, right there in one of the biggest rattlesnake concentrations in the country!

josephusflaviussolo@gmail.com

FACTOID: After our government ordered tons of new pennies to be manufactured, we managed to end up with an estimated $70 million dollar loss after production. The cost to make one penny was $.02 cents. After the pennies were manufactured and sold at face value, you and I are the ones that will pay the remaining $70 million debt. Maybe it will "rain and rain" and we'll all get "pennies from heaven" to cover the debt?

FACTOID: In 2011, the U.S. Government gave $2.6 million of our tax dollars to Eastern Europe for "parliamentary strengthening." That money taught Eastern Europeans how to balance and follow a budget! Is that something like paying a guy to teach cockroaches to play guitar? Who in the world did the United States Congress use to figure out how to balance our budget? Oh, now I get it. It was the shit throwing monkeys that taught them!

A few more Factoids:

Our friends in the north, sometimes referred to as the "Yankees", used slave-trading money to build factories that made war materials to defeat the South in the U.S. Civil War. And, we don't have a yearly celebration called "Thank A Yankee Week?" (Oxymoron or a Paradox?)

NASA is developing a machine to purify urine to be used as drinking water for astronauts? Count me out on that one.

A few more for the road:

- Porn takes in $57 billion a year. The government spends about $100 million every four years to subsidize parties at the political conventions. I do not know if these two issues have anything in common.
- The Department of Agriculture spent $2 million to fund an internship program. The program hired one full-time intern.

- Last year, $120 million was paid to dead federal employees.
- A total of $146 million was paid for federal employees to upgrade their flights to business class.
- The U.S. Government spent $2.6 million to encourage Chinese prostitutes to drink more responsibly.
- The Department of Health and Human Services provided an $800,000 subsidy to build an IHop in Washington, D.C.
- The National Institutes of Health has given $1.5 million to Brigham and Women's Hospital in Boston to study why "three-quarters" of lesbians in the United States are overweight and why most gay males are not.
- During 2012, $25,000 of federal money was spent on a promotional tour for the Alabama Watermelon Queen.
- The U.S. government spent $505,000 "to promote specialty hair and beauty products for cats and dogs" last year.
- NASA spends close to $1 million per year developing a menu of food items for a manned mission to Mars even though it is being projected that a manned mission to Mars is still decades away.
- Over the past 15 years, a total of approximately $5.25 million has been spent on hair care services for the U.S. Senate morons.
- The U.S. government spent $27 million to teach Moroccans how to design and make pottery in 2012.
- During fiscal 2012, the National Science Foundation gave researchers at Purdue University $350,000. They used part of that money to help fund a study that discovered that if golfers imagine that a hole is bigger it would help them with their putting.
- A total of $10,000 of U.S. taxpayer money was actually used to purchase "talking urinal cakes" in Michigan.
- Vice President Joe Biden and his staff stopped in Paris for one night back in February. The hotel bill for that one night came to $585,000.

- The U.S. Department of Agriculture has spent $300,000 to encourage Americans to eat caviar produced in Idaho.
- The National Institute of Health recently gave $666,905 to a group of researchers that is conducting a study on the benefits of watching reruns on television.
- The National Institute of Health also spent $592,527 on a study that sought to figure out once and for all why chimpanzees throw poop.
- The IRS spent $60,000 on a film parody of Star Trek and a film parody of Gilligan's Island.
- Last year, the federal government spent $96,000 to buy iPads for kindergarten students in Maine.
- The U.S. government spent $200,000 on "a tattoo removal program" in Mission Hills, Calif.
- Last year, the government spent just under $1 million posting snippets of poetry in zoos around the country.
- The U.S. Air Force Office of Scientific Research spent $300,000 on a study that concluded the first bird on Earth probably had black feathers.
- The federal government spent $75,000 to promote awareness about the role Michigan plays in producing Christmas trees and poinsettias.

Chapter 10

GIVE THE KID A PILL

FACTOID: It seems like everybody needs a pill, especially the children.

- 8,389,034 children are taking psychotic drugs in America.
- 4,404,360 children are taking pills for ADHD in America.
- 2,165,279 children are taking pills for depression in America.
- 830,000 children are taking anti-psychotics in America.
- 2,132,625 children are taking pills for anxiety in America.
- Over 18 Million American children are taking a pill for mental problems each day.

DISCUSSION: A Physician's Desk Reference (PDR) can be purchased on the web from $6 dollars to $80 dollars. The PDR is a dictionary for the 1,500 plus prescription pills and capsules for nearly every affliction known to mankind. Every day, new drugs are being produced and I'm thinking it won't be long before we run out of new names to call them. I take great pleasure in watching the numerous television commercials advertising their pharmaceuticals. I am not a couch potato but no one can escape the scads of television advertisements. To make matters worse, by the time they get done advertising the drug, I'm thinking I probably need to take one! And then logic and reality steps in and darned if somehow by osmosis, I start experiencing every one of the side effects they're constantly warning us about. I find intense hilarity over all of the side effects! The side effects we are cautioned on cover just about every side effect and symptom known on this planet. Suffice it to say that if you are still breathing after downing one of those pills, you better give your doctor a call and let them know you're still alive. Of the prescriptions I do take, there is no way I will sit there and read through the countless tiny litany of side effects and symptoms because I usually get them all. The warning data on most drugs is so long I could read "War and Peace" faster. In the 1800's, good 'ol snake oil did the trick. It cured every ailment with a guarantee of no appreciable side effects other than dead. I remember my mother coming home after shopping one day and she pulled out a bottle of vitamin pills and said, "Here Billy, you're going to start taking one of these pills every day." At 10 years of age, I felt I was old enough to ask "what for?" Mom quickly responded by calmly telling me that Ricky's mother was at the store and said her son "hasn't had a cold in 970 years" (or something like that), and "you're going to start taking one too." Seeing that mom was in a fair mood, I figured the matter was still open for discussion, so I exercised my 10 year old maturity once again by replying with a sarcastic, "oh, sure, now I have to take a stupid pill because of Ricky, who lives down the street!" I had never heard of laser beams at the time, but I can assure you that when I said the words "oh sure", old Doris's eyes suddenly had gone from a congenial roundish almond size to instantaneous snake eye slits, and two red fiery beams of some form of hot plasma began shooting outwards long enough for me to experience the heat and smell of burned hair! This convinced me that I needed to go ahead and start taking that One a Day pill. Good 'ol mom. She was always the one I would choose as my wingman for any air to air combat in a fighter jet with the enemy. By God, if she couldn't shoot them out of the air, she would go snake eyes, light up those laser beams of hers and melt those bad guys to a mound of hot jelly! I never liked Ricky again after that; of course, I never really liked him before the pill.

CASE IN POINT: It seems we're quick to denude a high spirited child with a drug. I don't know if children were created different when I was young, but I do remember a number of boys and girls who seemed to operate at much higher energy level than others – myself included. Some of my "pills" came in the form of discipline or a darn good spanking. But, for God sakes be very careful to spare the rod with your child. Now days, the children learn about child abuse at an early age and spankings are considered some form of child abuse. Years ago, teachers vectored a lot of a child's energy towards more projects of interest. I do not remember children in my class who needed peeling off the walls for being so hyperactive. Only in the last 20 or more years have I witnessed this condition. Is it the candy and sugars or the fast food or diets in general that are contributing to this dilemma? Or, is there simply a mass generation of parents who are so busy with their careers, there's not enough time in a day to spend quality time with a child? I do know that sometimes children will even cry and throw tantrums or scream for no apparent reason other than to simply be noticed. Kids are smart. They learn early on that any attention is better than no attention at all, even if they have to be bad to get recognized. I am not sure that teachers have the time to supplement the lack of love and attention children are not getting at home and are quick to point out there may be a psychological issue with the child. Indeed, there may very well be, but a pill to otherwise denude an extremely active child seems unfair and possibly unwarranted. Before that doctor is so quick to prescribe a pill, he or she might want to know a little more about the child's home life. Although I care not to go into any detail about my personal childhood, the problem may not be the child at all and could be the parents' who are contributing to most of the child's problems. One mother I know of is a screamer. She feels the child only responds when she screams at him. It didn't take long for dad to scream at the child too. Soon the child began doing the same things their parents taught them and started screaming back at his mother and father, and he became a problem in school. They have him on pharmaceutical drugs now. In the meantime, the mother thinks she's done the right thing. When this child was hauled into the doctor's office, it was the emotionally unbalanced child that began having problems in school and at home, surely not mom or dad. In most cases the child's true issue is lost in infinity, and has no advocate to support their quandary. Well, the child's mind is denuded with pharmaceuticals now and mom and dad don't need to take any pharmaceuticals, because apparently, there is nothing wrong with them. The parent's still scream and the boy remains to be dumbed down with a pill that helps him not to think. It's frustrating when the mom and dad are relatives of mine. In this case, these two parents are brainless professionals, bringing in top echelon salaries as dad is a doctor and mom is a physical therapist.

Do the parents know their child's personal Vitamin and Mineral Levels? If the human body is deficient in only ONE vitamin or mineral, a child's physical and mental health could be in danger, the immune system is compromised and I digress.

If only ONE Vitamin or Mineral deficiency exists in your child's body, do you know what it is?

josephusflaviussolo@gmail.com

Chapter 11

———❧———

BACKPACK BLUES

Apparently, those states that decided to legalize the lottery, thinking the schools were going to benefit must have had visions of grandeur. Schools are still using children to raise money for them. The school children are all encouraged (or coerced), to become little entrepreneurs whether they want to be or not. Gifts like backpacks with some cartoon space character are waved in front of the child's mesmerized faces and they're sent home to lean on mom, dad, grandma, grandpa, all of the aunts and uncles, cousins and friends to make as much money for the school as they can. Of course, the kids are placed on sales pressure thinking they will never raise the funds required by the school. But good 'ol mom and dad or the grandparents come to the rescue because there's no way the child will be penalized by not raising enough money for the school to get a dumb backpack just like all of the other kids will get. What really tans my hide is the schools know it too. What a travesty. I can't fathom the schools still use this technique of imposing that kind of tactic on the children. What does it teach? Does it teach children to be good negotiators or finance managers at an early age, or beggars? It seems these schools can raise enough money without placing the children in a panic that they might not qualify to get one of those backpacks. School administrators should be ashamed of themselves. You administrators should have your teachers learn how to fill out a grant request, and encourage them to come up with new and innovative ways to raise money besides preying on its school children and making them beggars. Is it fair to have an occasional fund raising event? Of course, but not the kind that requires a child to raise a set amount of money for the school before he or she may qualify for a goofy little backpack. As far as I am concerned the school system is taking advantage of children in the same way that was finally identified as being against the law years ago. Does child labor law ring a bell? It wasn't long ago that bad people were forcing deaf people to beg for money by walking around giving cards away. The deaf people were exploited just like children in schools are to this day. So stop it.

josephusflaviussolo@gmail.com

FACT: A grammar school in Lincoln, California just completed a "fun run" and all the school children participated by running several times around in a big circle. Those children who had the most money received from "the sponsors" (mom, dad, grandma, pa, etc.) got a special surprise from the school. One child's wealthy mom "sponsored" her child and gave $500.00. At the end of the run, of course, only the children who raised a ton of money were given a free ride all around town in a great big white limousine funded by the school. The rest of the children remained in their classrooms and studied while the successful beggars were awarded a limousine ride. How nice. I seriously question what the "fun run" taught. And what did the select few children who rode around in an expensive limousine learn from you school administrative geniuses?

Chapter 12

———∿———

VIDEO GAMES

My grandson calls it gaming. We didn't have video games when I was a kid. We spent most of our time outside in the fresh air riding bikes, playing baseball or basketball and walking around town with friends. We could do that back then. I don't remember having to lock or unlock a door or window in a house or car. I was free to drive my car most anywhere and never thought of parking my car in a safe area other than that one time I got in my car one night and sat on a sleeping homeless man's head! Is crime on the rise or was I oblivious to an evil world lurking around the public bathrooms, schools and parks like the perpetrators do today?

When I was a boy most of the men in their 20's, 30's and 40's were heroes. Nearly all the men and most of the women served in the military and didn't have time to become criminals. If their parents didn't teach them right from wrong Uncle Sam was right there to set them straight. Oh, we had our share of bad guys and gals, but not like the heinous horrible things that go on today with the unspeakable atrocities done to our American children. It's no wonder parents are quick to purchase video games where the kids are protected by staying at home in the house and safe, and not out on the street or in their own front yard for some freak to kidnap. Now, evil has entered all of our safe homes and seems to be permeating every mode of entertainment; and children are not exempt and become easy prey.

Video games started out with a tennis ball and two lines. Then it went to some funny looking brothers, to a bunch of monkeys and animals. Soon, there were worms that dug in dirt and space ships firing laser beams and little round-headed guys that made a really cool sound when they were caught and eaten. There were racecar games of all sorts and airplanes and jets that placed you right into the cockpit. All of these games seemed cool. Then Evil reigned. It wasn't long before parents could walk past the child's play station and see on the screen some unshaven character walk up to some person's car and pull the guy out and smash his face and watch the video blood splatter, then jump into the stolen car and drive away. It didn't take long before every kind of killing and violence came to the video gamers. Now, kids can communicate with other team members all over the world in real time. For example, in a military squad of five, one of the players on his play station can be sitting in his house in Sri Lanka, team player number two can be a teenager at home in England, team player three could be guy from Japan, team player four could be young man from Mississippi and team player number five from Alaska. It doesn't seem to matter what time zone they're in in any of these different countries because there are a lot of kids that can play on into the wee hours of the night and talk with each other in real time. Some of these games come with a 300-page manual that explains every detail of every kind of semi-auto pistol and caliber choices, a rifle, shotgun, machine gun or anything you can imagine is usually available. You would think the book was some kind of military technical manual. When all five team members are ready for combat, the kids communicate through headsets and begin their mission. That's when the fun begins. The team has a mission and the enemy is lurking from every window and door. All through the night, bodies explode, machine guns blow holes in every part of the body, blood splatters, heads roll off with every scenario of killing you can imagine. This activity becomes the order of the day for many kids. These kids are so used to taking part in video games killing and blowing up stuff, I would bet there are a lot of gaming children who are immune to the reality of true violence as it unfolds in our news broadcasts and in our streets. Many of these games are so close to reality I wouldn't be surprised that some of the kids could even suffer from Post Traumatic Stress Syndrome (PTSD). In the meantime, even more electronics become available like cell phones that can reach all facets of the internet, take pictures and text. It didn't take long for porno to flourish with a thing called "sexting" and children sending naked pictures back and forth in a text message. Kids today think they know more about sex than most of us parents, and they probably do.

J. SOLO'S SOLUTION: I don't really have a solution here, but I do have an opinion. If I were a young father I would be very hard pressed to go out and purchase bicycles or encourage the kids to go out doors to play in the streets and alone in public parks like we used to. I know I would be a hyper protective father and do nearly everything in my power to protect my children from all of the insanity we read about every day. Today, it seems like a world gone completely mad. My solution is best served by minding my own business on this issue when it comes to what should be done. However, before I could consider it a cold day before my child would take part in violent video gaming, I would have to monitor their computer every day, monitor their cell phone and monitor their texting somehow, then figure out a way to insulate them from the breeding grounds of pornographic evil, hatred and violence, and the worlds apparent mindset to corrupt every generation in America that has abandoned prayer and slapped God off the Throne. In the meantime children young and old, I feel that as our spinning blue marble continues on its path of downward immorality and self-destruction. A day will come where we will be faced with a time of horror that will make the most violent video game one could imagine pale to that of a cake walk in comparison. While we round up every gun in America with the thought of ending crime, we better gather up all of the knives, forks, ropes, chains, sticks, baseball bats, chair legs and rocks because as long as our laws continue to tolerate evil, the bad guys will find a way and our children will continue to be a potential victim.

josephusflaviussolo@gmail.com

Chapter 13

An Arresting Thought

Fact: Children are now partaking in mass killings. Some of these kids are making laborious kill plans and generate laborious ingress and exit strategy. Some of these kids know exactly how to load a clip, chamber a round and fire repeatedly at running targets. There is a potential that some student in a school near you is actively planning to go on a killing spree some day. And, all of this right under your nose, mom, and you too dad. Of course, you'll be the first person utterly shocked by the horrible news and wonder at what went wrong with your child. You won't be the first to know there were some indicators called discipline and respect problems. You know; the one's you've ignored or the issues that can't be ignored, but there is nothing you can do because you have already tried just about everything.

Discussion: The Bible has a story that addresses unruly children. The parents were instructed to take the child to the city gate to be punished by stoning. During Biblical times, the city gate was a place where the elders would mingle and conduct business. It makes me wonder at just how many children refused to conform to parental authority and were, in fact, stoned to death. I couldn't imagine that any child was stoned to death. I could imagine that many children who were taken towards the city gate had a sudden antipathy, and somewhere along the way the child began negotiating and talking like a magpie and making promises about what he or she would do to improve their disposition and attitude, and honor their mother and father.

Case In Point: A good friend of mine came to work one day all dressed up in a nice suit, carrying a long pale face. That afternoon he was going to a funeral. His wife's brother was killed by a 16 year old boyfriend. This man was a single father of a 14 year old girl who hated school, ran away all the time, had no respect or love for her father and used all variations of hateful anger towards the authority of her father. The father did everything he could to manage the home and provide for his daughter, but she would not conform to discipline of any kind. The daughter was in and out of school and suspended numerous times. She was placed in juvenile hall on a few occasions and her father called the police and pleaded for them to do something with his daughter for weeks on end. Authorities did nothing. One day, dad came home and his daughter asked him to walk down the hall towards his bedroom. When dad reached the bedroom, there was a 16 yearold boyfriend waiting with the father's own .38 pistol in hand and shot the father 5 times in the face and chest and he died on the floor. The daughter and boyfriend went outside and drove away in her father's truck. They were arrested 3 hours later in a small town 40 miles away. Three years later I heard the boy was still in jail and the daughter was released after 7 months and placed on probation.

J. Solo's Solution: Every time a child is arrested, maybe the parents should also get arrested. The arrest of the parents is a formality to officially place the parent on notice that their child has broken the law and was arrested. Each parent is booked and a $25 dollar bail fee is then paid by each parent, who will be immediately released from custody. Every time the child is arrested, his or her parents will be arrested. I can just about guarantee at some point the parents are going to get tired of a son or daughter's behavior. This is where "Adult Law" enters the picture. Parents should have an option to execute Adult Law when a child continues to defy authority. Every police station in America should have an Adult Law Form. The parents or single parent can warn their child that if they continue to stay out all night, hardly ever go to school and ignore the parent's authority, they will be subject to Adult Law. Once this form is filled out, that hateful child who defies parental authority will immediately fall under adult laws of the state. Let the child know what you have done and explain to them that because they think they're so tough, they now will be treated like an adult. When this child is arrested under Adult Law, the parent will not be arrested and is no longer responsible for the actions of their child. What this means is that if the 14 year old steals a car and runs over someone, he or she will be subject to adult laws and not juvenile laws. Juvenile Halls will be for children who have not reached their 12th birthday, commonly known as their age of accountability.

Another addition to the disciplinary issues of a child might be the introduction of a new "Ultra Advanced Scared Straight Program." From now on, every child who is placed in juvenile hall will be required to watch a video and pass a test. If the child cannot answer certain questions about the video, he or she will be required to watch it again and again if necessary, until they pass. The video is comprised of all actual executions recorded during chemical venous execution, electrocution, firing squad or by hanging or stoning. Each test is a series of questions the juvenile must answer correctly. As an example, one question might be "What color of shirt did the man wear when he was hanged?" Or, "What color were the shoes of the person that was electrocuted?" Correct answers on each test will insure the juvenile did, in fact, watch and pay attention. The reasoning here is if they pass the test, it is proof the videos were watched closely by the juvenile delinquent. This will be an effective program to serve as a constant reminder that if any juvenile delinquent intends to live a life of crime, he or she too, will become a future video candidate for execution. Scare them straight if needed.

josephusflaviussolo@gmail.com

Chapter 14

———————— ∽∽ ————————

CALCULATE THIS ONE

Fact: We are still teaching math with pencil and paper. But isn't there a better way?

Discussion: I suppose it began with bones and rocks. The quickest form of defense came in the form of a rock for me when dogs were in close pursuit. While in kindergarten I learned to count to six real fast. Every day I walked home, four different dogs were waiting out on the road for me to walk past. I carried two rocks in each front pocket and one in each hand. Those other 2 rocks served as extra ammo. It didn't take teachers long to begin showing us how to add, subtract, multiply and divide on paper. So, what the heck was a calculator anyway? The big kids carried these ruler units they called sliding scales and I wasn't sure I needed to get involved with those things when I grew up. I learned about the abacus and the mechanical calculator developed in the 17th century, but it wasn't until about 1970 before I saw my first hand held calculator called the Texas Instruments TI 30. By the end of that decade, calculators became more affordable and common in schools. Calculators can perform a host of tasks such as scientific calculations, SPC values, trigonometry, algebra, statistical process and graphing calculations, etc.

Case In Point: How many of us can still do square root, algebra, SPC, calculus and trigonometry without the use of a calculator? A calculator can solve a complex math problem instantly and it's accurately displayed within seconds. We all know this, so why are we still teaching the old methods of pencil and paper math? Why would a child be required to memorize his or her times tables?

J. Solo's Solution: Calculators. We have credit card sized calculator, many watches have the capability, our cell phones and computers are equipped as well. I agree that the basics of math should be known to the child, but if calculators were used right from the start, there is no reason why a 3rd grade student couldn't perform algebra, complex math and statistical calculations without difficulty.

josephusflaviussolo@gmail.com

Chapter 15

GOLDEN COUNTRY 1973

In 1973, a new country formed on planet earth. It was appropriately named Golden Country. This country instituted a governmental system that promised the laws, much like our own, would be strictly adhered to. However, unlike America and some of the other countries, when a crime was committed it was swiftly dealt with in a manner of such severity that the only fear that existed in this country was the knowledge that crime didn't pay. As a result, Golden Country lived in truly secure society, the kind we had here in America when I was a kid. No one needed to lock doors during the day or night. Women were comfortable outside at night and never feared for their safety. Parents never had reason to worry as their children played outdoors in their yards, rode bicycles to town, went on hikes with other young friends and never had fear of walking to and from school. Golden Country had the highest per capita income of any other nation in the world and unemployment was nonexistent. There were no homeless people and hunger was unheard of. Poverty didn't reside in Golden Country and because of its wealth and form of government all families drove a new car and truck every year. Each family was able to afford any hobby it chose. Golden Country was the wealthiest country on earth and gave freely to help all of the other countries in need. Many representatives and presidents of other countries flocked to Golden Country in an effort to learn more about its form of government. This form of government was a type of democracy based on a financial system that incorporated all the necessary checks and balances to ensure that every facet of their budget and spending was easily audited in a manner that would instantly detect any type of wrongdoing. Golden Country had a democratic system much like we have in America, except Golden Country citizens had the exclusive rights to vote on any and all laws, monetary changes, amendments, investing and all other forms of business. So, there was no need for senators, representatives or lobbyists. As a result, no one could be bought and no special interest group could influence a vote over its citizens. This society flourished as the country grew stronger each year. However, some of the representatives continued to flock to Golden Country 1973 in an effort of eagerness to learn more about the secrets of its success. Many nations followed suit and even adopted Golden Country's overpopulation solution. During the first 10 years, the people in other countries were becoming more informed and aware of a life of abounding success that boasted of safety, security and fabulous wealth. As the revelation began to unfold, some of the other nations became acutely aware of the cavalier attitude Golden Country had as it dealt with their solution for overpopulation, and their secret soon became ever and increasingly unpopular. It wasn't long before Golden Country became a pariah to most of the earths' inhabitants and the nation faded away into the shadows of obscurity and guilt as the annuls of history will forever remind us of its nightmarish horror of evil, which incessantly pervades the human mind.

What Happened? Golden Country 1973 was fully aware of the detrimental effects of overpopulation. All of the other countries suffered with overpopulation and Golden Country sought to resolve the issue before it became a problem. As this country formed its governmental laws it addressed and identified overpopulation as one of the primary causes of monetary deficit. Their government was sure that overpopulation was the primary contributor to hunger, poverty, abortion, crime and mass unemployment.

Golden Country incorporated a solution to overpopulation that was drafted as Law and was adopted by the citizens in 1973, and read as follows:

~~~

The Golden Country 1973 Overpopulation Solution: All newborn infants will be fingerprinted and kept on file in Golden Country government computer archives. This program will involve every child up to 10 years of age. Each month the government computer will randomly select fingerprints and names of those chosen, and inform the parents of all children selected and identified for disposal. For those children who were randomly selected, who are between the ages of birth to 10 years of age, the parents will be responsible to ensure custody of the child is rendered to the government agents for disposal. Body parts will be utilized as the government deems necessary to prolong the living. In the event a child reaches his or her 10th birthday and was not chosen for our overpopulation solution disposal program, we welcome you to a long and prosperous life in our society.

~~~

Well, as time went on in Golden Country, the pariah nation continued to prosper in its wealth and was able to ignore the atrocity of their solution to overpopulation. Many mothers and fathers, however, were devastated as random selections sadly interrupted their lives with grief and disparity when their own child was selected by the computer for disposal and subsequently handed over to government authorities. The grieving parents had to understand this law was voted and approved by its citizens. Since inception of the Golden City the statistics of the overpopulation disposal program were tallied from 1973 to the present, which culminated in the following:

- 2.5 children were disposed of every minute
- 150 children were disposed of every hour
- 3,600 children were disposed of every day
- 25,200 children were disposed of every week
- 100,800 children were disposed of every month
- 1,209,600 children were disposed of every year
- After 10 years 12,096,000 were disposed of

From 1973 to the present date the nation known as Golden Nation disposed of (killed), 50 MILLION children.

J. SOLO'S SOLUTION: Hold your heads up high America. You and I are the Golden Nation. It's called Abortion in America since 1973. We have successfully killed and disposed of 50 Million children since 1973. We (myself included), have a lot to be proud of, and that's my opinion. When I was a young married man predisposed by selfishness and pride, I felt I commanded all authority and it was me who was the chief engineer on my train of worldly life. I was a young married man who, in all of my blatant arrogance and ignorance, would not have hesitated to select abortion as an option. It was then I realized I didn't crawl out from under a rock 677 bagillion trillion years ago like some of our lofty genius ones would have us believe. Somehow, we've successfully slapped God completely off the Throne. How many mothers or fathers would willingly walk their 10- year old child over to a disposal facility? If not, how about a 9 year old or 8, maybe a 7, 6 or 5 year or 1 year old precious child? How about the "1 year option", where we can keep the parasite for up to one year and if the kid is too much of an inconvenience, we can shove them in a night drop for the government to dispose of later? Did you know a baby hears our voices 56 days after conception? All of the organs in that tiny body, are functioning and has the cutest, most precious one of a kind fingerprint you ever saw. Remember the "Start a Heart" program for heart attack victims? Well, a precious tiny little child's heart begins beating within 22 days of conception. If you think there just might be a higher authority or God, take a look around at this America of ours today and our prideful hearts might see the hand of God and His blessings, drift farther and farther away from this planet and on into oblivion.

CLOSING THOUGHT: Just think how many of those 50 Million children may have grown to become the very scientist that developed the cure for Cancer, or Diabetes, Alzheimer's and a host of other diseases? It's too late now to think about that, huh? Since 1973, who was thinking anyway?

josephusflaviussolo@gmail.com

Chapter 16

———— ⚮ ————

SPEAKING OF ABORTION

To ALL females. I am on your side, so read on.

FACT: Since 1973, Abortion has been legal in America. We all know the statistics as to how many. But, is there another suggestion out there? Well, I have one.

DISCUSSION: I have nagging questions:

- How many people does it take to cause pregnancy?
- How does the Male Sperm Donor get off scot-free after being party to an unwanted pregnancy?

Now, I may be a little old fashioned, but most pregnancies occur as a result of having sex between a male and a female. For those of you sitting on your brains in the Supreme Court, that means when a man and a woman have intimate relations. If required, maybe the old fossils at the Supreme Court should have a mandatory show and tell between themselves and see the difference of the sexual parts between a man and a woman, or talk about it together so they all understand. Many times intimate relations cause pregnancy. Since 1973, millions and millions of children have been aborted for convenience. The woman has the exclusive right to abort the fetus – not the man.

Fathers have contested a woman's right to have an abortion and the problem went all the way up to the Supreme Court. It was decided that the woman has the rights and the man (male donor – you know, the one with the penis, the other half of what it takes to cause most pregnancies), does not have any right of choice at all. Here's another example of "rights" we don't have:

Using the following illustration: An intoxicated man drives through a red light and slams into a car driven by a pregnant woman, killing both her and the fetus.

Before 1973, I would fully agree that the man killed two humans. The way the law reads now is the man can be found guilty in the deaths of two people. Now, this is where it gets confused.

So, how did the intoxicated man know she was or was not going to have an abortion? Why is he charged with killing two human beings, when the courts agree that "it's just a fetus; a parasite and isn't even human until just before birth"? Is it the woman, once again, that determines whether or not the fetus is a parasite or a human, making the man guilty of killing one or two people? So, let's change the scenario just a bit and use the same story again:

An intoxicated man drives through a red light and slams into a car driven by a pregnant woman, "who was on her way to a "Planned Parenthood Clinic" to have an abortion."

Did the man cause one person's death or two?

Well, the Supreme Court says two died even though the pregnant woman was on her way to have an abortion.

Let's turn the table around for just a moment and look at this man/woman = pregnancy, under a different set of circumstances. What if the 1973 courts ruled that only the male sperm donor could authorize an abortion? Wow, what a firestorm that would cause. Women would be burning more than their bras on that one! Now, think back on those same two examples of the intoxicated man running through a red light? In both of those cases, the father, man, sperm donor would make the ultimate decision as to whether the accident resulted in one or two persons being killed. Okay all you women out there – if that were the case is that a classic example of bigotry and unfairness or what?????

Now for you men out there called fathers, mannish sperm donors, and includes those of you who could care less about who you get pregnant. I am one of you. Do all of us males realize just how much we have had it made since 1973? Somehow, we have successfully brought about a law that places every bit of responsibility and accountability on every pregnant woman. The man doesn't have to worry about morning sickness, mood swings, cravings or put up with a swelling stomach, weight gain, ugliness and several doctor visits. WHOOOO HOOOOO!

And just think, while the "little woman" is all fat and ugly, us males can go out and find some more women to share our sperm with! Hey, and if you're not married, kick this one to the sidewalk because it's open season dude! You don't owe her a thing.

If something appears out of balance here, let's take a "Through the Looking Glass" approach.

Hoarse Sense: Every male who causes pregnancy should be accountable and responsible to the woman who is just as accountable and responsible to the man. To those of you sitting on your brains at the Supreme Court, I'm stating that both man and woman are EQUALLY accountable and responsible for that pregnancy. Every woman seeking abortion should be required to have the signature from her male donor to ensure that both the man and woman are taking responsibility of the decision to abort. Why? Because far too many women are required to make a monumental decision whether or not to abort a child. You have made a law so that every bit of that accountability and responsibility lies directly upon the woman's shoulders. Why should it be just her decision and let the man run off and donate sperm elsewhere? One of these days, logic will rule out over "stuck on dumb", and the law will be changed so that both the man and woman share the decision 50/50, when it comes to a decision to abort a child. If the 50/50 law were enacted, I think we would get tired of those irresponsible men and women who make a career out of pregnancy through welfare by being an unwed mother while happy boy just hangs around the house like a parasite. It's about time we started catching up with those male sperm donors who could care less whether a woman gets pregnant, and merrily skip away to chase another skirt while being exempt by Supreme Court Law of accountability or responsibility. You would think there might be a system that would require a DNA sample confirming both the mother and father before allowing any future abortion. If the law required DNA confirmation before any and all abortions, I would bet there would be fewer abortions and fewer unwanted pregnancies and fewer women that have to bear the guilt the rest of her life for having to make such a horrible monumental decision. It wouldn't take long for little happy weeny to run out of money paying his dues for all the children he is responsible for. Let's make men monetarily responsible for the fun they have. Make men pay for their half of the abortion, make men responsible for their half of the decision for abortion, make men accountable for their half of the unprotected sex habits. We might want to be careful, however. If we were able to enact a 50/50 law, those brain sitters in the Supreme Court might also change the law when it comes to the man driving through a red light and slamming into a car killing 2 people. Who knows, maybe the ruling on that one after the 50/50 law would find him guilty of killing one and one-half persons – how utterly senseless and cavalier we have become.

josephusflaviussolo@gmail.com

Chapter 17

---∽∾---

GPS Wristat

FACT: The Global Positioning System has been a useful tool in providing the user an unsurpassed accurate location nearly anywhere on earth. Once reserved for military use only, it became available to the private user. Automobiles, hikers, boaters and pilots of airplanes use the GPS system for navigation purposes. Using up to 6 space satellites at any given time, exact measurements are far more accurate than those of late. GPS tracking devices are also used by the authorities. In California, there were about 8,000 parolees and felons (mostly sex offenders or gang members), wearing these devices strapped to their ankle. If the wearer tampers with the unit, tries to run from authorities or gets too close to a school or other unauthorized area, he or she is subject to apprehension. However, reception can fail in those instances where buildings or cell reception is intermittent. One investigation found that thousands of child molesters, high-risk parolees and rapists were removing or figuring out a way to disarm the tracking devices. Most of the perpetrators were not arrested because the California jails and prisons were already "too full to hold them".

In any given state, over 800 Americans have spent time in jail or prison per 100,000 people.

DISCUSSION: Use of the GPS as an alternate means of keeping our jail and prison populations low is a great idea as long as a tracking device can be designed to be tamper proof.

CASE IN POINT: In California, two major contractors competed for the GPS tracking system for prisoners and after countless amounts of money were spent, they both failed miserably. Ample research and evaluation was not taken proactively and after "thousands" of prisoners were fitted with the tracking device and released, it took the parolees no time at all to bias the system and render its tracking capabilities useless. Then, to make matters worse, after authorities found the tracking devices were easily compromised, authorities realized the inflated cost it would take to round up the bad guys and place them back into the prison system. It was then that the mindless wonders (authorities), further realized that once all the bad guys were caught, they couldn't put them back into the overcrowded prisons for heck sakes; that's why authorities let them out wearing the GPS tracking devices in the first place!

J. SOLO'S SOLUTION: Employ a man or woman as the focal point. He or she will be responsible for the oversight of a tamper free ankle GPS tracking device that has been tested extensively, by every means possible. Then, submit the GPS tracking device to Myth Busters and let them have some fun on TV trying to figure out a way to beat the device. Oh, and do all of the testing and work all of the bugs out BEFORE you strap these on thousands of parolees to go hog wild in suburban America. Personally, I feel there should be a mechanism that stuns the crap out of anyone trying to mess with the GPS tracking device once it has been placed onto the ankle. The tracking device should stun the wearer a total of three times, then the ankle GPS tracking device explodes and tears off the foot and the ankle. That way, the bad guy or gal won't be too hard to chase down. Once the perpetrator is located, a new GPS tracking device will be fitted around the neck – well, you know where I'm headed (pun intended), with this one. Hopefully, coming to a city near you is the next subject.

josephusflaviussolo@gmail.com

Chapter 18

―――――∾∾――――

THE EXPLOSIVE NECKLACE

FACT: Crime in America does pay. If you don't believe that fact, take a ride on the Web and peruse the studies that will confirm that crime and penalty are so unbalanced it's pathetic. In some cases if you have enough money you can kill 4 or 5 people in a car and get off with probation.

DISCUSSION: We all know how overcrowded the jails and prisons are and the problem isn't going to go away anytime soon. As long as laws are diluted and money seems to lessen the penalties, there will be more and more prisoners filling the prisons of the future.

CASE IN POINT: There are currently thousands of people serving their time in jail and prisons. Many of the high crime or potentially recurring heinous types could be wearing the GPS tracking devices as well. In many cases, that's just not good enough.

J. SOLO'S SOLUTION: Molesters, murderers, rapists, heinous criminals, repeat offenders and all other violent criminals should be fitted with an Exploding Necklace. All high crime offenders will be permitted to serve their prison time at home. Their prison cell becomes their house and yard. A tamper free device is installed beneath the surface of the yard perimeter. In the event an offender walks close to, or across the perimeter line, the necklace will detect the violation and emit a loud ear-piercing wail. In the event the offender ignores the audible warning for a period of 30 seconds and makes no attempt to return to the inside perimeter, the necklace explodes. If the criminal has no home, the government will provide one for him. If the criminal has no family to make food preparations, one of our U.S. delivery companies will deliver a weekly box of provisions. In the event of a medical emergency, local authorities will have the means to shut the necklace system down. Because the criminal has elected the Home Prison privilege, another 10 years is added to his or her prison term. In fact, let's get rid of all of our U.S. prisons and contract them out to other countries. That way, we wouldn't have to pay so much money to feed, clothe and maintain our own prison systems. So, other than death row inmates, most all other prisoners have two choices. Either serve your time at home with a nice shiny necklace or you can serve your prison time in another country. By the way, congress will not perform any oversight at the foreign prison facilities. The Federal Government spent $750,000 dollars for a new soccer field for the detainees held at Guantanamo Bay. Aren't we nice? OK, so each Home Prison will have a basketball hoop over the garage and a ball will be provided. However, should the ball go outside the perimeter it is hoped the prisoner can retrieve the ball and get back in time before the head begins to ache from the long term results of the explosion.

josephusflaviussolo@gmail.com

Chapter 19

PUNISHMENT TO FIT THE CRIME

STORY 1

FACT: On a road, somewhere between Tracy and Modesto, California, the nightmare of terror began. It was in 1978, and many of us have forgotten about the 51- year old former merchant seaman by the name of Lawrence Bernard Singleton, who picked up a 15 - year old hitchhiker. After he raped her, he used a dull hatchet to hack off both of her upper arms above the elbows and threw her naked bleeding body from a road, down in a culvert 30 feet below to bleed to death and die. The teenager somehow survived. At some point later, the naked bleeding 15 - year old girl made her way up onto the road and a passerby rushed her to a local hospital. Mr. Singleton was sentenced to a whopping 14 years in prison and was released from a California prison after serving only 8 years for rape, kidnapping, mayhem and attempted murder of a child.

DISCUSSION: Here is a classic example of leniency, stupidity and our inability to use common sense. When the California Prison System let the scumbag out of prison, he made his way to Florida. In 1990, he served 60 days for theft of a disposable camera and then served a two-year prison term for stealing a hat. In 1997, a neighbor called the police to report an assault. It was Singleton again. This time he was successful in murdering Roxanne Hayes, a mother of three. Singleton stabbed her multiple times in her upper body.

I lived in Sacramento in 1978, and vividly remember the gruesome and callous crimes of Mr. Singleton. I was in a state of shock when stuck on stupid people let him go after serving only 8 years in prison. I couldn't believe the prison system could allow a monster of his caliber any kind of freedom. It was nearly 20 years later that I heard this man's name again. This time, it was the nightly news coming from Florida, where a known criminal by the name of Singleton, who decided to attempt murder again. I also felt my head explode when one of the news media pencilnecks stated the murdered woman was "just a local prostitute." It didn't take long before I learned this was the same man that raped and hacked the arms off of a 15-year old girl outside of Modesto, California, and left her to bleed and die.

CASE IN POINT: Where is the justice here? After serving 8 years in prison and released, the prosecutor stated "Mr. Singleton had no remorse, did not accept responsibility; and if anything, he is worse now." Well, the system let him go anyway, and who should be surprised he did it again? The 15-year old teenage victim received a civil lawsuit settlement of over 2 million dollars that was never paid and she is currently spending her life with artificial limbs and has to use her feet for most chores.

Singleton didn't have any money and she never received a penny from the lawsuit she won. Well, the outrage in California caused legislation to require a term of 25 years to life. Big stinking deal. Of course, the law took place AFTER such a heinous crime was committed.

J. SOLO'S SOLUTION: Isn't it time we instituted a law of Punishment to Fit the Crime? In the case of Lawrence Singleton, both of his arms should have been hacked off using the same hatchet he used on the teenage girl. Then before Mr. Singleton bled to death, he should have been rushed to a hospital to receive whatever medical services he requires to ensure his survival. After this man is healed, he should have been placed back in his prison cell until at some point later he begins to complain about not being fed. When this guy gets hungry, a prison guard will simply throw part of one of his own frozen arm sections in the cell and ask if he would like some water to help wash his meal down. After this guy has run out of "arm" food, it's time for the same dull hatchet to remove the legs. Sound gruesome, heinous and terrible? Yes it does. But, how many more horrible crimes do we need before we ever get the attention of the criminal and the present justice system? There seems to be a systemic problem here. What deterrents are there when dealing with bad guys? Bad people do bad things because nothing bad ever happens to them after they've done the crime! I suppose you could come up with your own punishment to fit the crime when it comes to rape. I remember a mother who strapped her children in the back seat of a car and let it roll down a boat ramp and into a lake to drown her own 3 little ones. If that mother was found sane, she should have been strapped in a car and drowned to the point of a near death experience at least 9 times. Then, on the 10th time, leave the car and scumbaglet in the water. Oh, I almost forgot to tell you what happened to Mr. Singleton. After he murdered the mother of 3 children he was sentenced to death for the murder, but the coward died of cancer before his sentence was carried out. This pig lived for 74 years.

STORY 2

This crime takes place in 1991, in Los Angeles, California. A 19 year old was secretly videotaped beating a 2-year old girl on the forehead with a wooden spoon. Judge Richard E. Spann viewed a five - minute segment of the videotape, which showed a sobbing little 2 - year old girl trying to fend off blows to her forehead, while Nanny struck the child on the forehead several times more. Nanny, was in America illegally from Mexico. The little girl's father became concerned and suspicious about his daughter's behavior. Each workday, mom was the first out the door and every time dad would kiss his daughter before leaving, the little girl would begin screaming and the big tears just wouldn't stop flowing. Dad finally got suspicious and put piece of black tape over the bright red recording button on a stuffed animal. Dad activated the video camera on top of the television set, went to work and left it running. That evening, dad and mom watched with anger, rage and horror.

What happened to little Nanny? Not much, but maybe it's good that I am retired. If I had been in Judge Richard E. Spann's shoes, I would have ordered a full workup on her blood to see if she is not seriously lacking any Vitamin or Minerals in her system, because some serious deficiencies can cause a very unstable mind, and I would have ruled that out immediately. The second thing I would have done is appoint a Structural Engineer to perform a video impact study of the 19 year old inflicting those hurtful blows to the forehead of the 2 year old child. The engineer could easily compute the woman's application of the force with the spoon she used to beat this child on the forehead. Results of the engineering impact study would determine the exact comparable force the Nanny would receive as punishment. For instance, if the child weighed only 37 pounds at the time, the study would accurately depict how much force and how big Nanny's Spoon is going to be (depending upon her weight.) After the study is complete, the comparable spoon fixture would apply the very same beating, force and duration on Nannies forehead as was inflicted upon the child. Except this Nanny would be required to attend a total of 10 separate forehead beatings, using the adjusted force proportionate to and frequency as she gave the child. In addition, this young lady would be spending some solitary confinement in a jail. Yes, I would try to be as fair a judge as I could, but she would be required to serve several months of weekends sitting in jail. Hopefully, that would get her attention. Also, the Nanny would be required by the court to open an education account on behalf of the victim child and pay a set fee each month toward the victim's education for the rest of her life. So, here's the deal Nanny. You will be taking a sum of money out of your pocket for the rest of your life due to your anger, ignorance and stupidity. Lady, you don't know just how lucky you are. If I had been serving as your judge, you would most certainly have paid your due diligence with a "Punishment To Fit the Crime", times ten.

Okay, I welcome my reader's comments. You can be polite or nasty if you wish. I would appreciate any and all corrective criticism, or reasoning for your case. I will respond to you in a civil, logical manner and your comments will be given the utmost respect.

josephusflaviussolo@gmail.com

Chapter 20

———❧———

THE TRUTH ABOUT SERUM

The Supreme Court ruled in 1963 that confession statements made by people under the influence of truth serum drugs was "unconstitutionally coerced" and threatened citizens rights under the fifth amendment, so it was declared inadmissible. Sodium Thiopental (a.k.a. Sodium Pentothal $C11H17NaO2S$ was discovered in the 1930's.) Some of the common side effects of Pentothal include hiccups, sneezing, slow heart rate, sleepiness and some shivering. The words "unconstitutionally coerced" actually threatened our citizen's rights. Isn't that what took place during the COVID 19 epidemic? Weren't citizens coerced and threatened to take the series of vaccines? Weren't parents threatened their children would have to be vaccinated to attend school? Were we forced to wear a mask against our will? Wasn't it our country that has imposed several coercive acts against U.S. Citizens in its shameful history? Does anyone feel it's time to take another look at crime? Some believe an accused person is coerced when their rights are taken away and forced in to a one way mirrored room and interrogated for hours. What is wrong in seeking the truth? What if this society did use Sodium Pentothal to find the truth from some known criminal and then should we proceed to waterboarding for confirmation? Where are our citizen rights when crime in this country runs rampant and allows/ tolerates crime to run hog wild?

Where are the rights for the victim and loved ones who suffer when a crime is committed? Seems like we all have our "rights". The government decided to give all WWI veterans a whopping promissory note of $1.25 for every day they served in the war. Uncle Sam called it a "Bonus" and all of the veterans were told they would be paid later………. in 1944. A depression got in the way and people everywhere were in a very difficult monetary quandary. The WWI veterans went to Washington to see if they could cash in their $1.25 bonus bonds. Nope. It isn't 1944 yet "so beat it or else!") General Douglas McArthur was summoned by the president and told to take care of the "bonus vets". Yep, they sure did. Major Dwight D. Eisenhower was there with his Army troops and Major Patton was there with his tanks to "take care of those veterans." They killed two veterans and burned down all of their living quarters and our American history of facts are enshrouded in a dark cloud of shame. No lessons were learned from its dark history and no shame was admitted. Instead, the issue became swept under the rug of political shame. The Supreme Court didn't protect their citizen rights, but if you're a veteran be careful your not coerced out of your homes. There is much more to say about these WWI veterans and their account that will be covered in depth later in the book. Shame on U.S. We should be proud at the way we treat our veterans. I am a disabled combat American veteran and I know what coerced means. Since 1885 the Statue of Liberty has proudly displayed her torch of "Enlightening the World" and "Lady Justice" proudly stands and wears a blindfold and carries the scales of Justice and armed with a sword with questions that still need to be addressed:

- What was the real purpose of the Civil War? What is the definition of Civil?

- Fleeing from the throes of WWII and Hitler, can someone explain why Jewish immigrants were not welcome in the United States, but forced to turn their ships around and "go somewhere else." The rejected Jewish Immigrants who didn't have a home or a country were given only a glimpse of the Statue of Liberty from the ships as they sailed away from anywhere but here in the land of freedom. Freedom huh.
- Why has it taken 157 years to finally placate our black citizens with a "Juneteenth" holiday?
- Why were WWI veterans and their families coerced in Washington by an unfriendly military force?
- How did the Tulsa Massacre happen? Who were the racist white ones that killed hundreds of black people, burned their homes and businesses in the Black Greenwood district and left thousands homeless in Oklahoma because they were jealous and well to do? Why were the local police and National Guard out there killing and burning everything, along with the rest of the white hostile mob? Who were the private pilots that dropped large gasoline bombs on the black people in Tulsa?
- Look at what we've done with our Native American Indians who were rounded up by the military and forced away from their homes and land? I stand corrected – we let them have casinos now. Whooped de doo.
- Besides, America broke only 500 of their treaties and still nothing is being done in the way of justice.
- How about those 120,000 Japanese citizens, who were ordered from their homes and placed in mandatory "internment camps" for 3 years (a.k.a. concentration camps according to the dictionary.)
- Who were the many government doctors who performed illegal sterility surgeries on nearly every woman when American Indians came for other medical reasons in our American history? So much for the Hippocratic Oath to "do no harm." Was

the government money just too good to ignore? Be proud doctors, including my doctor son-in-law.

I could go on and on. What I don't see is a country that is fair to all of its citizens, yet the Supreme Court jumps into high gear to protect the rights of a potential criminal.

I think Jack Nicholson had it right when he told a young-military prosecutor in a movie, "You can't handle the truth!" Where is justice and truth anyway? Computers have been a great source of research for me and when I was young, I had a lot of questions that were questionable about our history and politics and now I get it. When I was younger, my encyclopedias and school books were all I could use as a resource. Now, thanks to computer technology, a plethora of information is out there and at our disposal. Research and seek the truth for yourself. Select any of the 8 topics I addressed or choose your own subject you've been thinking wasn't right all these years. Imagine the possibilities if all of America's citizens knew the truth about a lot of America's forgotten or ignored lies, fake news and failures that were swept under the rug and abandoned like an orphan child.

josephusflaviussolo@gmail.com.

Chapter 21

STONED ON DEATH

Over the many decades of time, Americans have been arguing about Capital Punishment. The act of electrocution has outraged a number of citizens as well as death by hanging and death by injection. Each one of these punishment modes seems to cause a lot of American people to think the punishment of death inflicted upon a murderer is cruel and unjust. Well, be sure to tell that to the next victim's parents after their child was raped and murdered unmercifully or their arms were cut off and left in a culvert to die. Or, let the grieving parents know how terrible it would be that the rapist and murderer might be placed on death row, and how he or she should not pay for the crime and be held in a prison still breathing air, eating food, watching T.V., reading books and working out at the prison gym every day. Oh and who knows, some day the prison system will just let them go free anyway. Some say, "Can't we just show mercy towards the murderer and let the prisoner breathe air until death from old age?" Who is paying to feed and house the murderer? We are.

A life for a life. We need to start thinking about what the bible has to say about the condemned. Capitol Punishment was death by stoning. Let's consider having a newly improved version of Capitol Punishment. In this instance, the rapist/murderer would serve his or her time in prison with a mandatory day job. Each morning, the prisoner would be taken out to a stairway of an elevated Grain Hopper designed for the "Stonee". Grain Hoppers are still in use in America. A truck can park beneath the hopper, and the grain dumps out of the bottom of the hopper's outlet and into a truck bed. The prisoner's job every day will be to carry rocks up a spiral ladder to the top of the Grain Hopper and toss them in. If the prisoner refuses to carry rocks up to the hopper, he or she will not be fed. After a few hunger pangs, the prisoner will be more than motivated to complete his or her day job of filling the overhead hopper with rocks. When the Grain Hopper gets full of rocks, the "Stonee" stands beneath the gate valve and even gets to pull his or her own cord, opening the gate valve and viola! The rocks will plummet the condemned and form a nice, tall rock pile. Punishment of Death by Stoning is complete. The rock pile will remain as a testimony to the crime committed. Of course this includes the making a documented video of the event for the upcoming future criminal kids to watch when they go to the Scared Really Straight Program. Is death by Stoning biblical? Yes. Indeed it is. And no, I don't think they were using Grain Hoppers back then, or trucks or video. The "video documentation" during biblical times was recorded in a Holy book no one wants to read or follow because hatred, prejudice, greed, power and money prevails in a world that has turned its back on God.

josephusflaviussolo@gmail.com

Chapter 22

OLD BARTENDER RULES

My dad was a barfly. He enjoyed going to his favorite bar nearly every day after work. After retirement, he continued frequenting bars. He told me a story about a young 30ish Bully; a rooster of a man, who staggered in the bar one afternoon, grabbed a stool and shinnied up to the bar after a measure of difficulty, and ordered a whiskey and water. Everyone in the bar could tell the young man was visibly over served, and the old bartender explained to the young man that he was sorry, but it appeared he had had too much to drink already and offered the man a soda or water. This made the young drunk furious, and as he nearly toppled over during his stool dismount, he started some kind of a shadow boxing exercise prance dance out on the floor in his dusty red boots. This dude was shouting and yelling like a wild maniac, and challenging patrons as they scattered away to hug the walls, just like in the movies. It's amazing what too much drink can do and this kid thought he had the strength of Goliath. The old bartender began waving his arms and telling the young man to, "leave and get the hell out of here." That's when the young rooster bellered out just like old John Wayne did in Rooster Cogburn! Instead of leaving, the young bully turned to accept what he thought was a challenge to fight the old bartender! As the young man staggered, bobbed and weaved towards the bar in his drunken stupor, his intentions were to launch himself up over the bar with the help of one of the stools. Before the dancing fool was able to launch over the stool, the old bartender came up with an aerosol can of flying insect spray, and stopped that 220-pound cockroach dead in his tracks! Dad told me the drunk took a good spray of that stuff "right in both of his eyes!" The drunken boxer quickly changed from an angry fisted bobber and weaver to a low crawler, who dropped straight to the floor, temporarily blinded by the flying insect spray. Goliath the goon was still lying on the floor digging at his eyes when the police arrived. What a great way to protect yourself. When my girls began driving their own cars, both of them had the best of the best flying insect spray in their car. This stuff was as mean as a junkyard dog, and could reach out to about 25 feet! The one I insisted the girls kept in their car was the kind that boasted of "43,000 dielectric volts" of stopping power. I have sprayed this at yellow jackets in flight, and as soon as the spray hit their bodies, they did a nosedive straight to terra firma. So, to all of you drunks or bullies, I am glad you never intimidated one of my girls while they were in their car. I'm not sure if my girls are still carrying a can of that spray in their car, but they probably should because you just never know. Then again, I might be a little jumpy or paranoid after being shot at outside of a bar in Ethiopia, Africa, and shot at flying Huey helicopters during combat missions in Vietnam. At my home, one can of wasp spray usually sits on top of the refrigerator, and one can is posted near my wife's bed. I've even taken a can of that flying insect spray along for an angry bear or mountain lion while hiking in the Sierras of California. So, did I, or my family ever have to defend ourselves with the flying insect spray? Heck no, not yet......... But, I can assure you that all of us are secure at the home front. So, go be a Goliath and bother someone else you can bully. Your next match might be a deadly mistake.

josephusflaviussolo@gmail.com

Chapter 23

———✀———

PROTONS AND NEUTRONS

Cars and trucks used to have distributors. Distributors became extinct and were replaced by solid-state ignition systems. Back then, those old distributors provided an intense spark of energy through each wire connected to a spark plug. The energy spark ignited the compressed mixture of air and gas in each cylinder, which created the locomotion necessary for the car to roll forward. Every one of those old distributors had a small cylindrical device called a capacitor (also known as a condenser) and that's the focus of this subject. The little capacitor had one little wire coming from the top of it and some of us kids found that if you took the wire and shoved it into the spark plug receptacle and cranked the engine over a little bit, you could pull that capacitor out of the receptacle, throw it to one of your friends and watch the fun. I always made sure I was stronger or could easily outrun the guy because once the little capacitor and the wire touched his hand, a gigantic burst of electrical shock jolted the testosterone right out of him! The first inception of a unit that stored energy like a capacitor was discovered in 1745, by Ewald Georg von Kleist, from Pomerania, Germany. Less than a year later, Dutch physicist, Pieter van Musschenbroek invented a functional capacitor. Pieter was so impressed by the tremendous power yielded by the electrical shock he sustained, he stated, "I would not take a second shock for the kingdom of France!" In today's world, we have low-voltage, electrolytic, solid state, variable polymer, high-energy units, supercapacitors and new technology on the way.

CASE IN POINT: Do you have any idea why the human body jumps completely off the table when a heart defibrillator unleashes its electrical charge? Those two pads placed on the human body, are shocking the heart into a restart, with up to 10,000 volts and every muscle in the body instantly contracts! Here is another example I want to share with you in hope the word "capacitor" becomes an indelible reminder of its energy potential: Did you know a small, disposable camera flash unit powered by a tiny little 1.5 volt AA, which contains only 15 jouls of energy, can instantly convert that little flash unit to a burst of over 300 volts, which is easily capable of delivering an enormous electrical shock like a stun gun? And wouldn't you know it, it didn't take us long to figure out how the Military Industrial Complex could develop extremely high energy Pulse Energy Power weapons like Rail Guns and Coil Guns.

J. SOLO'S SOLUTION: Once again logic hit the back burner. We're so preoccupied with making some kind of weapon out of laser technology, no one cares to give its potential any consideration to provide Americans a free "energy resource or potential." Haven't we figured out how to destroy the earth, its moon and the rest of the galaxy with the weapons we already have? President Ronald Reagan revealed the Strategic Defense System (SDI) on March 23rd, 1983, and was known as Star Wars by the news media. At the time, I was a government agent monitoring contracts for the SDI projects at a large rocket motor plant in California. SDI was real, and the defense system used a transpiration cooled nose tip (TCNT), attached to an endo-atmospheric destructive interceptor (HEDI) missile capable of speeds of 260,000 mph. America's updated defense shield has been changed to high energy laser beam technology and could be easily modified to power earth-based capacitors. So, the space based laser platform could include a large capacitor and would also serve an additional purpose to provide inexpensive, low cost energy as well as its primary mission to destroy enemy nuclear missile launches from any hostile country on earth. Billions of American dollars were funded and the technology morphed into use of stationary high altitude energy laser beam platforms instead of missiles. Now days, we have exo-atmosphere kill vehicles over 311 miles up in space, lingering in stationary orbit, waiting to destroy an enemy missile launch. Our earth receives a constant solar radiation level from 50 watts to 250 watts per square meter per day on this earth, even after being diluted by our magnetosphere. However, the heat and radiation levels at thermosphere altitudes, would heat capacitors installed at each of the laser platforms beginning at 311 miles to 621 miles above earth, depending on the temperature desired. Stationary orbit capacitors, equipped with laser transport in our thermosphere can produce heat ranging from 250 degrees centigrade (400 degrees Fahrenheit) up to 1,700 degrees centigrade, (3092 degrees Fahrenheit). Metals that can withstand these temperatures are Platinum, Rhodium, Nickel, Molybdenum, Tantalum, Thorium and Tungsten. Imagine a space based energy capacitor and a laser beam transferring all of that free energy from space to a Stirling engine here on earth. How about if America makes peaceful use of those laser guns in space, by providing free energy laser energy bursts from the onboard space platforms to fire a high energy laser beam at an earth-based capacitor, which transfers the energy to a large Advanced Stirling Engine. The engines have one moving part, and can run continuously from 14 to 17 years before requiring replacement. (These are the same engines that are capable of generating electrical energy from high radioactive thermal heat coming from our 70,000 tons of nuclear waste that will be sitting around doing nothing for the next 240,000 years, (refer to Nuclear Stuff #2).

All of our stationary orbiting laser weaponry could easily absorb heat and radiation that can be beamed to capacitors on earth, powering the Stirling engines. The sun produces solar thermal radiation, which is part of a large collection of energy called the electromagnetic spectrum. The sun's radiation produces heat, visible light, ultraviolet light, radio waves, X-rays and gamma rays. However, exo-atmospheric levels of solar thermal radiation would be greatly enhanced from space altitudes. It can be used as a limitless source of continuous energy, instead of just using the laser weapons to melt incoming nuclear missiles from an enemy country. However, while the threat of an enemy launched missile exists, their secondary usefulness could be used to power earth-based capacitors. I am not advocating we eliminate the weapon base capability in space, I am saying we should make dual purpose use of the laser platforms, and when they're not used for enemy missile launces, they're busy beaming down free energy from above. America could have a gigantic source of free energy, so turn on all of the lights and rejoice. While we Americans are waiting to flip the switch of free energy resource from the sun, we could encourage our president or congress to hold off on destroying mankind with advanced weaponry and start those same minds on a new path that isn't so preoccupied with destruction. I want to point out the usage of the word as applied to the sun is not really perpetual. I only mean for the next 10 trillion years, because science has told me the sun is supposed to shine that much longer. Suffice it to say it's a little longer than you Congressmen and women, who make your job of not doing much of anything, an entire career.

josephusflaviussolo@gmail.com

Chapter 24

WORLD HUNGER

World Hunger: Did you know 8,000 children each day no longer go hungry? That's because 8,000 children die each day because of starvation. Hunger never advanced in this generation, knowing every single day 8,000 children die, while Earthlings pour countless trillions into our military industrial complex and weapons of destruction, space programs, global warming and terrorists, busily preoccupied with killing each other in the name of a religion. Oh well, that's really only 240 thousand deaths each month. Without looking to blame any of the other countries on this Earth, how about us Americans? Do we have a Specific Purpose Bond that might help to feed these children and fund these nations with whatever it takes for them to begin feeding themselves in an effort to rid the problem of world hunger? In 1970, America and the worlds' richest countries agreed to give 0.7% of their Gross National Income for International Aid, which includes world hunger. Well, guess what nations topped the charts way over and above the 0.7% target? Thank you Norway, my hats off to you Sweden, way to go Denmark, thank you United Kingdom and the Netherlands too!

I am sorry that my country, America, has fallen morbidly far, far below the agreed 0.7%. We're even lower than Iceland, Japan, Canada and even the tiny nation of Portugal. These other nations need to realize we just don't have the money after what the Gore Global Warming has done to us, and how about that Fannie Mae and Freddie Mac blunder that caused us to borrow from China? And then there were those Middle Eastern war issues we had to almost win that cost us a lot of money; but at least we won't have to bother with them again, right? Then there's our National Debt of over 38 + trillion dollars that none of us here in America have any idea how we got there. So, those of you that are still hungry can just wait until we get all of our debts paid off. Maybe we can send you some pills or something that will help to stave off hunger. Maybe those dying children are the results of overpopulation or something. We have a program here in America that takes care of most of the children that go hungry – it's called "Abortion". I'm thinking if we send over a plane load of Congressmen to see the starving children die, then have countless congressional insight meetings and spend a billion or two to let them study this issue for themselves for the next ten years. They may get through all of their pomp and circumstance and countless TV interviews long enough to make even more empty promises. I know, let's steal it out of the Social Security moneybag! In the meantime 2,880,000 innocent children starve to death each year, as this great nation of ours spirals down the sewer line unable or unwilling to fund our fair share of 0.7%. I'm not interested in revolution; I am not advocating any form of communism or socialism in America. I'm just looking for democracy in its fullest; the day America can be strong again, responsible again and think more logically when it comes to our budget, financing, politics and Law and Order. Would a Specific Purpose Bond for World Hunger have any relevance in this case? History continues to demonstrate evil and greed flourishes in all facets of life. We all have seen the forces and effects of monetary greed in our experiences with relatives, siblings, businesses and organizations. In each case, I have been reminded of the old adage to "Follow the

Money." One could only ponder the thought that greedy fingers right here in America could be the reason why we have fallen so short of our commitment to give at least 0.7% towards the effort to pay our fair share and end world hunger. Indeed, the full amount of money may very well have been given but when the moneybag gets to the World Hunger designate, someone may have already helped themselves to a large portion. As tomorrow approaches, with but a few hours away, the dawn of 8 thousand more children will die of starvation. Our political leaders in America should be proud. We all know who our leaders are; they're the ones that are exempt of Obama Care, and exempt of our serf health care system. Somehow, the elite of America are exempt of the laws you and I have to follow, exempt of having to drive their own cars and having never experienced the reality of mounting bills and food prices, while trembling hands cover the worried faces of mothers and fathers who are agonizing each month over just how you and I are going to make ends meet each month. I recall one president hopeful who won the election, boastfully expounding the word "Change". Really? He was not to blame. U.S. is. I firmly believe the U.S. Government was organized with all of the necessary checks and balances to function properly. Somehow, somewhere along the way, American politics got lost in greed and lawlessness. So there, I said it, and now I think I feel better. At least, until the next 24 hours brings in a new dawn, and with it the echoing sounds of the crying, empty stomachs of more dying children as its dirge of hunger permeates my heart strings with sorrow, reminding me of those empty stomachs and small crying voices again, each and every day. What will tomorrow bring other than more death, sorrow, fear and more hunger?

josephusflaviussolo@gmail.com

Chapter 25

MEMORIES OF OLD

Let's start this story with a few questions. Would you give a man all of your money if he told you he used to be a bank robber? Would you allow a person known as a child molester to drive your children to school? Would you give the enemy top-secret information about nuclear fission? Would you give monetary support to a terrorist group? Well, way back in the early days, most folks were driving mule trains, covered wagons and buckboards. In those days, kids that lived far from the nearest school rode in on horses. In just a hundred years, technology has taken us to new dimensions. Who would of thought that 119 years ago an airplane was designed, built and flown by two bicycle repair shop workers, and 126 years ago a guy named Henry Ford came up with a car. He not only revolutionized the world with his innovative Model T Ford, he began a technique called mass production. That event changed the entire manufacturing industry. Ol' Henry was a thinker well beyond his time and offered the buyer any color of the spectrum as long as they liked black, because that's the only color that was offered. Ford products thrive to this day as a leader in the manufacturing process of cars and trucks galore. I do have one problem with Henry though, and I want to be the first to tell you I own a Ford SUV. But, in spite of Henry Ford's brilliant abilities and innovation, he considered Hitler a hero. In fact, Henry Ford even donated tons of money towards the Nazi movement and proudly displayed a picture of his hero, Adolph Hitler, in his office. Of course, Mr. Hitler thought so much of Henry Ford, he too, kept a picture of his friend, Henry. While Senator McCarthy witch hunted all the alleged communists out of Hollywood in the 40's and 50's, a young movie director by the name of Alfred Hitchcock was dispatched to film and document the horror of what the Nazis' inflicted on the 6 million Jews. Hitchcock's cameras recorded the frail Kwashiocor bodies of those who barely survived the horrors of the holocaust. Henry continued building us cars – and wouldn't you know it, American citizens bought them and he prospered by making tens of millions of dollars. I find it interesting how money can change a person. What I find most interesting is how easily we forget the wrongs or just ignore them completely. In my case, I too, have joined the wooly flock of the mass of sheep that ignores what Henry did during the war, and continue driving those Fords along with all my fellow sheep who are still purchasing Ford products, knowing that it all began with one man who had a better idea. All of his generations have profited and live in Henry Ford's luxury. Yet, marred by the generation that supported and helped sponsor a crazed man who tortured and exterminated countless men, women and children, which, by doing so, resulted in a terrible war that killed and wounded tens of thousands of American soldiers. The wheel of time dilutes the mind as it fades away into obscurity, so who cares about details anyway? Henry Ford wasn't the only one and there's no need to drone on about what Bayer was doing during WWII and General Motors and many other industries who played both sides of the war to insure their survival and fed their greed by profiting from both the enemy and the United States. America should be proud.

FACTIOD: It's strange that rubber tires were invented by accident even before a car was even thought of and the natural color of a tire is white and not black. They use dye.

josephusflaviussolo@gmail.com

Chapter 26

CHILDREN'S LIVES MATTER

Someone tell me WHO doesn't think Black Lives Matter? White lives matter, red lives matter, yellow lives matter, brown lives matter and green lives matter. Color has nothing to do with it! If God made us all color blind, we could all be just one happy family, right? I seriously doubt it.

What it has come to is that DISRESPECT for others and disrespect for authority DOES matter. Children's lives matter, but when children are brutally murdered in their schools I don't see a throng of people burning up cars, breaking windows, vandalizing stores, rioting in the streets, throwing bricks and shooting at policemen. Peaceful demonstrations yes, I am all for it. But this insanity of opportunity to go wild in the streets to steal and destroy property and senseless killing has got to stop. Where are you rioters when children are killed in their classrooms? And, there are city officials planning to defund the police?

Disrespect for others and disrespect for authority DOES matter. It started with our parents, so think about that. I can go on and on about why all lives matter. I challenge anyone to come up with a solution.

Stop the violence. Do something peaceful and intelligent and come up with a peaceful and better solution.

Peaceful demonstrations are welcome in America. Does something need to be done with those who take advantage of authority like some crooked police, congressmen, teachers, federal, state, county and city officials and the general public do? YES.

This nation just had a policeman with authority, who placed his knee on a black man's neck and attributed, if not directly caused this man's death. This is an example of pure madness fed by hatred. Unfortunately, this country does not punish authority when it gets out of hand. Does this officer deserve the full punishment of the law? Yes, of course. The real question here is causation. What caused the officer to restrain a person in a manner that would cause death? The question is: Could physically resisting arrest, spitting in a policeman's face, throwing rocks, stealing merchandise, breaking windows, burning cars, tearing down statues, killing police officers and causing weeks of violence be a definition of the word "defying authority?" Look in the mirror fellow citizens, countrymen and women. What a shameful, disrespecting, ignorant race caught up in the name of prejudice (all colors), we have become here in America! It seems it doesn't really matter anymore, and maybe we should revert back 200 years, and all of us should carry guns, including all school children. Now that would make sense in today's world I suppose.

The problem is authority. Do I respect authority? Yes, if the discipline is according to our system of laws and respect is dealt both ways. I demand respect and so do you.

"All acts of those in authority will show respect at all times to all people. All acts of the people will respect authority at all times." Do you disagree?

SOLUTION:

I don't know the short answer to this and maybe you do. Let us begin with RESPECT. Discipline breeds respect and respect breeds love.

We must ask ourselves if we defy the authority of God, do we know and understand that the consequences will be just?

Likewise: Hold accountable those who are in authority and taking advantage of the common people. Hold accountable those who are defying authority. In the case against this police officer, also hold accountable his authorities above him. Who thought up this manner of constraint and who authorized it? Let's focus on authority and question its intent instead of responding with violence.

How do we as a nation, get the attention of anyone defying law and authority? Well, for those who are in authority, you better make sure every person who enacts that particular authority, is fully trained and are following finite procedure because you will be held accountable. For those citizens who defy law and authority, I have an opinion:

Let's start a "New and Improved Law System." This law system is based upon a child's future driving privilege. A license to drive a vehicle should be predicated on how well the child grows to maturity. If the child grows up with a history of disobedience and defiance at home, school truancy or bad grades and a prior police record; is there someone who can explain to me why the hell these people are driving 7,000 pound cars and trucks? If children express a desire to grow up stupid, they will stay stupid and should never become a licensed driver by their own admonition and undoing.

Imagine the future of what this New and Improved Law System could do for a peaceful society. It would:

1. Drastically reduce accidental and purposeful death, (unqualified drivers are driving bikes instead of cars).
2. Less bank robberies. Bicycles don't go fast.
3. Less crime. Bicycle "get-a-ways" are easy perps to follow.
4. Quickly reduce road rage.

A child's normal history of maturity level would dictate whether or not the young adult would have a driver's license. Gross disrespect and defiance of parental or lawful authority = loss of license. Every citizen who defies just law and authority in the home, in school and in the public could be subject to loss of driving privileges. If a person of authority or a common citizen defies authority that involves criminal disrespect of authority, whether they are a cop or not should probably drive a bicycle.

Parents responsible for minors who defy authority should also be held accountable in some manner. I don't think anyone can tell me they didn't see, suspect or know the symptoms.

So feel free to kill, destroy, steal and burn if you so choose, but you will be pedaling a bicycle for your getaway vehicle.

In the meantime, parents living in California are the ones signing for a 16 year old when it comes time to driving a car. If a son or daughter is a druggie, has a history of attitude problems at home and at school, what are we doing signing authorization for the kid to drive in the first place?

If my opinions seem callous, wrong or harsh, please let me know. I could use correction just as much as anyone.

josephusflaviussolo@gmail.com

Chapter 27

PEON OR PEED-ON

So, I sent this letter to Melania Trump. Most First Ladies champion a cause for humanity of some kind so I decided to do what I could for the common cause to address the issue of Crib Death. I suppose the clerk who opened the letter didn't feel the matter was significant enough. Maybe it was just another dumb idea of mine. Or maybe I should have included the many degrees and titles I hold, but I didn't feel the need to.

Galileo Galilei was a college drop out. He didn't invent the telescope. His daughters became nuns and he was sentenced to life in prison by the Roman Inquisition and spent his later years under house arrest. Galileo believed in heliocentrism, which is a belief that the Earth and planets revolve around the Sun at the center of the Universe. The Catholic Church believed in geocentricism, in that the earth was the center of the universe and all celestial bodies moved around the earth. So, Galileo was convicted of heresy in the courts of law, because his beliefs were contrary to religious doctrine, and he spent the rest of his life under "house arrest."

Dear First Lady Melania Trump:

After having read your official First Lady biography, I clearly realized your staunch desire to continue in your care for children as noted in your history of involvement regarding "Love Our Children USA", "National Child Abuse Prevention", and other interests in recognition of your dedication towards health and well-being of our children.

Hence, I will get straight to my point. **I am asking that you would champion a proactive Vitamin and Mineral Level program that could eradicate the Sudden Infant Death Syndrome (SIDS).**

Brief overview of what the effects of a deficiency of only 1 vitamin can cause. In this case, let's use a deficiency of Vitamin K:

1. In 1894, Dr. Townsend described 50 cases of bleeding in newborns, naming the condition "Haemorrhagic Disease of the Newborn" (HDN). Vitamin K eradicated the problem.
2. In 1930, a biochemist found that Vitamin K deficiency was the cause of baby chickens bleeding to death.
3. In 1944, a Swedish study involved 13,000 infants who were given 0.5 mg of Vitamin K on the first day of life. The researcher found that infants who received Vitamin K experienced a 5-fold reduction in the risk of bleeding to death.
4. From 1894 to 1961, a total of 67 years transpired before it was concluded that Vitamin K shots should be given to infants to prevent from internally bleeding to death. In 1961, after 2 decades of research, the American Academy of Pediatrics made the recommendation to inject the infant with Vitamin K.

Since 1961, Sudden Infant Death has been significantly reduced by injection of 1 simple vitamin. However, infants continue to die attributed to the Sudden Infant Death Syndrome. In fact, a 2009 Infant mortality rate provided by www.cia.gov reveals that of the 34 listed countries, the United States is ranked number 34. Americans have the highest infant death rate of 6.22 per 1,000 births. In the midst of current medical technological advances we have turned our logic reasoning away from the importance of maintaining optimum levels of Vitamins and Minerals.

Prenatal physicians are now involved in a very proactive effort towards pregnancy testing. Many tests do, in fact, monitor some vitamin and mineral levels and studies have resulted in the importance of the government's recommendation of including folic acid, vitamin D and other ingredients to be added to our foods.

But, these measures have not improved results, leaving the U.S. with the highest infancy death rate over 33 other countries. While countless millions of dollars are being spent on further research that will involve another decade or so, that same research forgot to look at one of the simplest of issues, that being Vitamin and Mineral Levels and its intrinsic importance.

CASE IN POINT:

In simple terms, my vitamin and mineral levels were inherited from my parents. My dad was a smoker and heavy drinker and Mom smoked. Research has proven that abuse of alcohol and smoking causes deficiencies in many vitamins and minerals. Logic concludes that when I was born in 1948, I became the product of my parents and received a combination of mom and dad's vitamin and mineral levels. My parent's vitamin and mineral levels were unknown. Hence, my inherited vitamin and mineral levels were unknown at the time of birth.

OBJECTIVE and PROPOSAL:

1. *Develop and perform a complete Vitamin and Mineral Level blood testing for volunteer prospective mothers and fathers at least 6 months prior to the anticipated pregnancy. Any*

noted vitamin and mineral deficiencies or overdose can be corrected prior to the anticipated pregnancy.

2. *During the pregnancy, perform Vitamin and Mineral Level blood testing to ensure the mother is at optimum levels throughout pregnancy.*

3. *Perform a complete Vitamin and Mineral Level blood test on each infant as soon after birth as is practicable. Supplement as required by doctors to achieve optimum levels.*

4. *Develop a program that requires complete Vitamin and Mineral blood testing on all deceased infants that perish as a result of suspected SIDS.*

That's it, Melania. Simple logic and maintaining optimum levels of Vitamins and Minerals will produce a baby that will start their life with the highest possible immunity system God has ever intended for mankind. I firmly believe infant death from SIDS will significantly drop. I pray you are motivated to consider my proposal. The V & M test could be annual or bi-annual.

Your program of complete Vitamin and Mineral Level testing and implementation of items 1, 2, 3 and 4 (above), shouldn't cost billions of dollars or take another 67 years of medical or scientific research. Please also consider the health and well-being of all Americans citizens if our NEW Healthcare System INCLUDED routine blood testing for infants, children, adults and the elderly that includes a program of maintaining Vitamin and Mineral Levels. Does it make logic sense that we would be a healthier country and ultimately save billions and billions of dollars using this simple proactive health methodology?

I sincerely hope that you take consideration and I would like nothing more than you receiving the Nobel Peace Prize for your accomplishments in the field of helping our children by your efforts to maintain their peak levels of vitamins and minerals.

CONCLUSION:

Not all is lost in the field of the importance of Vitamins and Minerals. A quick Google Search will reveal that Chickens and Beef are the most Vitamin and Mineral healthy beings on this earth. Extreme vitamin and mineral level research studies in the Poultry and Beef Industry has produced astounding results. These two industries maintain their poultry and beef Vitamin and Mineral needs at optimum levels. Do chickens and cattle get sick and die? Of course they do, but large producers of the Chicken and Beef Industry have their Vitamin and Mineral Levels to an exacting science to maximize immunity levels. Not so for us humans.

As you know, the medical profession does not perform routine blood testing for all Vitamin and Mineral Levels. While I am fully aware that most blood testing does include the monitoring of a "few" vitamins and minerals, we are told by the medical profession that "if we maintain a balanced diet, we should be getting all of our required vitamins and minerals". Melania, this is not true. Have you or anyone you know ever had a complete Vitamin and Mineral Level Blood Test?

In closing, I would like to thank you for your time. If I can be of further help, or if you need any additional information, please do not hesitate in contacting me at your earliest convenience.

By the way, I researched and found a Lab here in Texas that charges $390.00 to $420.00 for complete Vitamin and Mineral Testing Levels and was completely astounded by the results. I was deficient in 3 important vitamins and minerals, and borderline deficient in 9 others. I am presently taking supplements and will gladly pay for my next test in six months. My daughter now believes in the importance of maintaining optimum V & M Levels, particularly after my grandson was afflicted with leukemia. In my heart, I will always wonder if his disease could have been exacerbated due to a diminished immunity system caused by deficient levels of V & M. And, I do not believe that having optimum vitamin and mineral levels will cure the world of all of its diseases – however, let's at least take that extra step of logic and see what transpires. We did it with chickens and we did it with beef........ But for some reason, the extra step for humans was overlooked, ignored, or not seen as any value added.

May God continue to Bless you and your family and keep you safe.

William John Fowler
(At this point in my letter, I included my name, a short biography, address, phone number should anyone from the White House be interested in knowing more about the importance of Vitamins and Minerals.)

(End of Letter to Melania)

Comments: It has been 8 years since I received a typical, traditional common boilerplate letter they use for everyone that states how much Melania "appreciates letters." I am sure Melania never saw the letter. In reality, some clerk opened my letter, then filled out the boilerplate and mailed me my thank you letter with her stamped signature. I haven't heard a thing, and it has been 8 years. I was ignorant and expected that maybe someone out there would listen to obvious logic. However, I do feel like a common peon with too few credentials for the president's wife and staff to take any notice, or be interested enough. So, no more letters from me, as I fade away as a peon, or maybe I was just peed on, Lol.

Just so we all know:

Vitamin D deficiency causes rickets, joint and muscle pain.
Vitamin A overdose can cause death. Early explorers ate a Polar Bear's liver and died. Polar Bear liver is so high in Vitamin A it is extremely deadly toxic to humans even if you eat a small portion.
Vitamin A deficiency can lead to "night blindness".
Vitamin B12 deficiency is common in 10 to 20% of the elderly, with symptoms of decreased mental capacity and other neurological

disorders, (some doctors are prescribing supplement B12 to patients).

A Folate deficiency can cause or worsen mental difficulties. Case in point is a 1996 study of 177 elderly people and almost 50% had intake levels below recommended values.

In 1992, the World Health Organization (WHO) finally figured out that if they gave children of third world countries Vitamin B, they wouldn't go blind. It worked.

A Copper deficiency can lead to mental violence in men. So, are all prisoners screened for vitamin or mineral deficiencies that might have been violent attributed to a mental imbalance? Is this why there are so many nut cases in this world, capable of the most heinous crimes known to mankind? There was one study of prisoners who were given placebos and the other prisoners were kept at peak vitamin and mineral levels. It was found the prisoners who had maintained proper levels were far less violent, easier to get along with and caused lesser problems within the prison system.

Is it possible to even consider that most, if not all, diseases could be prevented by maintaining the highest levels of Vitamins and Minerals? Who knows? No offense to the medical industry, but why are doctors so quick to screen for nearly everything except maintaining Levels of Vitamins and Minerals, but instead do not hesitate in writing us a prescription drug while ignoring a possible V & M deficiency?

Has there ever been any research involving a link between children with ADD and Vitamin/Mineral Levels? Did you know that if any mother or father were to read about vitamins and minerals they would clearly understand that numerous mental issues in children are caused by vitamin or mineral deficiencies? Yet, doctors will stand in line waiting to counsel your child and prescribe a mind altering drug.

Were you aware that even though vitamins and minerals are the foundational basic and most essential necessity for healthy living, doctors apparently have no concern. If you ask your doctor for a complete vitamin and mineral level test, he or she will wonder why you should be concerned. After all, we live in America ("and a balanced diet will give us all of the vitamins and minerals needed to maintain a healthy body.") I guarantee your doctor will not rule out the possibility of vitamin or mineral deficiency/overdose, because they do occur. However, our current health plans have no provision for V&M testing, so the cost for the blood test is on our bank accounts and not covered by any health plan.

There is a case in Great Britain where a 6 week old baby was taken away from the parents and they were charged for child cruelty because the doctor noticed bruises that were thought to be fractures on the baby's body. Defense experts discovered the child was suffering from Von Willebrand disease, a blood disorder that causes a person to bruise easily, as well as a Vitamin D deficiency, which causes infantile rickets. The parents in this case were found not guilty through a legal process that took 3 years before mother and father were finally reunited with their child as a family again.

josephusflaviussolo@gmail.com

The sale of Supplemental Vitamins and Minerals, including a plethora of other stuff has profited this industry over 6 billion dollars each year. Somehow, Americans are quite proactive in purchasing every kind of supplement they can think of, and many do not understand the seriousness of possibly causing an overdose condition. Over the many years, I too, was guilty of purchasing vitamins and minerals nilly-willy without knowing my V & M Levels. I encourage all readers of this letter to ask your friends and relatives if they know their exact Vitamin and Mineral Levels. If they are taking a multivitamin, ask them "why?" Their answer will most likely be, "well it doesn't hurt to take a multi-vitamin." Now ask them why they shouldn't or don't smoke – they know the exact answer to this question.

Good ol' mom was proactive when I was 10 years old. She decided I needed to take a One-A-Day vitamin because "Rickey's mother gives him one every day." At the age of 10 I wondered for another 58 years before I stopped wondering and began research. I now know my exact V & M Levels because I pay for the results.

If anyone took the time to review all diseases, sickness and afflictions resulting in vitamin and mineral deficiencies or overdose, one may agree that it is possible God, did indeed create mankind in His image, and may have intended that we might become healthier if our systems included optimum Vitamin and Mineral Levels. To believe otherwise, would be to suggest His perfection in creation is flawed.

I am willing to pass the torch of data I have regarding vitamins and minerals, to any one of you readers, who may have an empirical interest in learning more.

josephusflaviussolo@gmail.com

Chapter 28

———✶✶———

VITAMIN A FOR ONE

Several studies show that vitamin and mineral content in the food we eat has been steadily decreasing and the pesticides and other contaminants have been rising. Even with Organics the soil vitamin and mineral content is still not what it was even 60 years ago. So to say that we get all the vitamins and minerals we need from our food is a fallacy. I strongly mentioned earlier in the book the claim that if only one vitamin or mineral was deficient in the human body it could have detrimental effects on the Immune System. The following information reveals consequences of deficiency or overdose of only one vitamin. Here is a long synopsis of what one vitamin or mineral deficiency can do: We will cover Vitamin A as one representative vitamin:

Vitamin A deficiency symptoms: Night blindness due to ulcers on the cornea, karatomalacia (softening of the eye cornea), impaired hair growth, loss of appetite, lowered resistance to infections, dry eyes. It is the leading cause of blindness in children (250,000 to 500,000 per year, half of the children die within a year of becoming blind) and increases the risk of child deaths, especially from diarrhea and measles as well as maternal deaths. Globally, 1 in 3 pre-school aged children and about 1 in 6 pregnant women are vitamin A deficient due to inadequate dietary intake. Weak bones and teeth, glare blindness (problems seeing in bright light), inflamed eyes, nausea, vomiting, loss of appetite, tiredness, weight loss, anorexia, anemia, altered mentation, headaches, dizziness, blurred vision, poor muscle coordination, itchiness and scaling of the skin, bone pain, irregular menstruation in women, osteoporosis (bones become weak or brittle), temporary or permanent liver damage, diarrhea or xeropthalmia (abnormally dry eyes). Vitamin A deficiency can be considered a nutritionally acquired immunodeficiency disease. Chronic alcohol consumption can result in depletion of liver storage of Vitamin A.

VITAMIN A - OVERDOSE SYMPTOMS

Death. Depression, blurry vision, cough, decreased thyroid functions, increased pressure in the brain, hair loss, indigestion, irritability, muscle pain, redness in skin, seizure, sore eyes, cracked lips, cirrhosis of the liver, mouth ulcers, stomach and intestine issues, increased risk of lung cancer, changes in the immune function, increased risk of heart related disease, conjunctivitis, joint pain, thyroid changes, respiratory infections, cracks in fingernails, delirium, diarrhea, vomiting, swelling or bulging of the eyes, coma, headache, fatigue.

Author's Comment: I guess we've all had or continue to suffer from some of the above symptoms and maladies and find there is no deficiency of Vitamin A in the body. I also realize the above symptoms of Vitamin A overdose and deficiencies are not going to be miraculously healed just by maintaining proper levels of Vitamin A alone. Visit your family doctor and request he order you a complete vitamin and mineral test – good luck with that. A proactive Preventive Medical effort is of paramount importance as it relates to a program that will follow and make adjustments for ALL of our Vitamin and Mineral Level needs.

So, the questions remain:

1. Do you know your personal vitamin and mineral levels?
2. Are you on a program that maintains your peak values of each vitamin and mineral?
3. Are you beginning to understand that if our bodies were continually fortified by a program that maximized our personal levels of vitamins and minerals on a sustained basis, how much more healthy and strong our Mental Health and Immune System might be?

It took a plethora of brilliant minds 300 years to realize that after scurvy killed millions of people, it was caused by a Vitamin C deficiency – a simple process of eating the right fruits and vegetables and now are available in pill form. You might want to research Vitamin C before your neighbor convinces you otherwise. Even the Japanese Navy lost many of their soldiers because no one knew that the lack of eating citrus and fruits aboard ships was their deadly nemesis. (Comments regarding any medical health practices or professional advice in this book is informational only. I am not a qualified medical practitioner or professional nutritionist. Seek medical advice from your health provider for professional advice.)

josephusflaviussolo@gmail.com

Chapter 29

———✁———

The Political Whores
of Civil War

In 1867, Joseph Lister introduced carbolic acid, which significantly reduced infectious germs. During the Civil War, there was a 90% amputation rate, even for a compound fracture. By 1875, sterilization of instruments and scrubbing of hands were widely practiced. Death rates were extremely high, especially compound fractures. Meanwhile, British and American surgeons were irked by the Scottish upstart according to Harvard University. However, it was Ignaz Semmelweis, who was first to require hand washing using carbolic acid in 1847, and the death rate went from 12%, down to only 1%. He was ridiculed, shunned by other doctors and died in an insane asylum. The prolific writer and medical doctor, Oliver Wendell Holmes was threatened he could lose his medical license when he suggested people might live longer if "us doctors washed their hands between patients." But the whore of pride and arrogance lingered on, and the Civil War inflicted 642,422 casualties, including 483,016 Confederate casualties. The Civil War killed more soldiers than WWI, WWII, Korea, Vietnam, and the Revolutionary war of 1812. ***Diarrhea was the leading cause of death during the Civil War due to uncleanliness.*** A total of 204,000 were battle deaths, another 413,458 lives were lost due to disease. Why such a high death rate due to disease? Most casualties were attributed to blatant lack of cleanliness, i.e., washing hands with soap and water. How easy this was to figure, but the whore of pride and arrogance got in the way. Who would have thought that soap and water was the simple key to cleanliness? Did you know that one bacterium can spread and reproduce 5,000 billion, billion bacterial germ microorganisms in one day? Unfortunately, the prideful doctors did not believe in germs, and I continue to bask in the enlightenment of reading all variations of "stuck on stupid."

I suppose it would be more fitting if one should ask the simpler question, "Who had the audacity to call Civil War a Civil War?" It wasn't civil? Couldn't us Americans have been more CIVIL about its problems that never would have approached the word "War?" First of all, war is not civil, and never will be civil. The word "Civil" means "courteous and polite." What in the hell was "courteous and polite" about killing 642,422 in a "Civil" war? Civil people are the ones that relate to ordinary citizens and their concerns, as distinct from military or ecclesiastical matters. How did the argument between the north and the south ever obviate itself and manifest in to a senseless WAR, and gravitate towards killing of masses of fellow American Citizens? The better question should be; "Did anyone from Congress contemplate asking what the black men and black women of America thought about slavery?" Hell No, they didn't! The true reason for that war was the whore of politics, and was not driven by remorse and conviction from the bonding of humans into positions of slavery. And the final result of that political upheaval resulted in more dead American citizens. The monetary riches transferred from the South to the Northern politicians. All one has to do is research and "follow the money trail."

So, here is what life, parents, teachers, and YOU taught me about the Civil War.

1. War used up millions of dollars. Who got the money? I want some!
2. Use deadly force and kill if you are in disagreement.
3. Slaves were free; but never free at all. The North made sure of that. Slaves would have remained as slaves even if the South had won the war.
4. Who made all the money from this war? It sure as hell wasn't about freedom from the bondages of slavery!
5. The words freedom from the bondage of slavery did not occur when the war was won and freedom never occurred until stupid people started thinking, so please keep thinking and change.
6. In 1865, nobody "won" anything. Someone else prospered and the manipulators were laughing all the way to the bank.
7. I never even knew what slaves were until you older citizens taught me with your books and pictures and showed me the "slaves" were all the black people. I heard all of your racial jokes.
8. My parents were great teachers! I listened and learned white lies, all about the black people, and I am too ashamed to tell you what I was taught.

8 X American's Money = Dirty money placed in someone else's hands who were not living as a true honest American Citizen, who were politically driven and determined to feed their desire as that of a common whore feeding on fame, greed, power and money and manipulation of the citizens.

The Sum of it all is greed. Think about that before your son or daughter goes off to fight a new war in a foreign land or if American politics decides we need to kill more citizens in the name of racial prejudice. Criminal Politics taught us prejudice.

Why didn't Congress ask the "slaves" what they thought? Why didn't Congress ask the black people, who were IN slavery what could be done with the problem of slavery? Do you suppose that if the blacks made the decision to abolish slavery they would have killed each other for freedom? Does that question even make any sense? The "slaves" President Lincoln freed, were simply placated and not given equal freedom like the other, lighter skinned "folks" in America already had. By the way, I don't remember going to school with any black people. I never saw a black person in my school until I was in the 8th grade attending Daniel Webster Junior High School in 1961. In 1966, I was in the military assigned to Fort Rucker, Alabama. So, 101 years after freedom was "granted" in 1865, I am sitting on a bus in Dothan, and there is a big sign inside above the front windshield with the following statement:

"COLOREDS SIT IN THE BACK OF THE BUS"

So, I get off the bus in Alabama, and run to a gas station and was shocked that it had 3 bathrooms with three separate doors with signs attached. "White men", "white women", and one that says "colored." All this country needed to do was look up north. Canada abolished slavery in 1834. They were too diplomatic and intelligent to kill each other and didn't split the provinces because of hatred and monetary gain. That's exactly why the people of Canada have a higher I.Q. than the people of America. Duh, and we wonder why? Other than looking up to how Canada resolved slavery without killing each other, maybe America forgot to really look up; to look up far beyond the Canadian Provinces, and out into the cosmos where God dwells and strive to follow His teachings. During the horror of a war between our citizen selves, including relatives and brothers against brothers, who made the decision for justified killing of each other? Congress? I suppose it would be easy for us citizens to blame Congress for everything. There is a problem, however, you and I are the very ones that placed these incompetent people in office to make such life threatening decisions of ignorance on our behalf. Did the soldiers that killed each other ever stop to think the only reason they were carrying a loaded rifle was because Congress wanted them to? How utterly insane. Next time, I strongly suggest us Americans consider sending Congress to the front lines to fight the next dam useless war. Let Congressional lives' bear the tragedy of death, standing there in a field with a rifle to settle America's problems. You politicians lead and we might follow. If we are not able to get along with other nations out there on planet earth, let's begin to look inward towards ourselves and research to learn our true history, and correct America's historical blunders. Lead, follow or get the hell out of the way. Our American history is not so bright and that's why WE are not so bright. If we were we would have looked UP to the God of this nation of ours, who was identified and known by our forefathers. As a nation we have morbidly fallen short of what is right and wrong and we don't know enough to recognize Him anymore. Us Americans have done a fine job of slapping God off of His Throne in our schools, in some of our churches, our universities, science courses, biological misinterpreted biased theorems, and a conundrum of physiological and psychological theories that obviate and obscure clear righteous thinking in our homes, our workplace, and in our marriage. These attributes feed the fuel of moral ineptitude. Good job, us! We should all be proud of our American heritage!

Hell, it took this America 157 years before the black people were given a Juneteenth Holiday! Whoop de doo doo! When the holiday comes up next year you can expect all the white people to take the day off too. Does that make any sense at all? When slavery was supposedly abolished, how come I still see legal instruments in a Texas clerk's office where slaves were still being sold AFTER the slaves were proclaimed as being freed?

In 1863, Abraham Lincoln signed the Emancipation Proclamation, activated the Union Army and freed all of the slaves in the "hostile" states of America! So, why didn't the Proclamation also become law to the American Citizens on the side of the North? Apparently, slaves were NOT given freedom in the North. Is that how our history reads? Juneteenth commemorates the end of slavery on June 19, 1865, when

Union Army troops from the north stormed into Texas, took control of the state and "freed all of the slaves." So, who was on first, when 25 states in the north, including five of those states in the north that "were in the process of abolishing slavery?" And when the slaves were freed in Texas, the "PROCESS" only took 157 years to fully recognize the occasion and nationally commemorate it. Okay, I get it too. I worked for the government for 38 years and Rip Van Winkle (a.k.a. Uncle Sam), was asleep most of the time. However, by gosh, Juneteenth is a great celebratory period for remembering that Uncle Sam was out feeding crumbs of false promises to the black citizens of America for 157 years and by dam, he finally remembered the slaves and granted Americans their own holiday in 2022! Good job Washington D.C.! Oh, and Uncle Sam, the color of my blood that surges through my body is the same color as yours and every person who was and is a slave and has a heart with blood the same color as yours, but you've been too dam busy looking at the color of the skin during every one of those 157 years, right? If our hearts and blood were different colors, would we show prejudice of that as well?

By the way Uncle Sam, when you needed more northern Union Army troops to fight your battle, you "baited" slaves living in the northern states with "freedom" if they joined the Union Army. If the North was fighting the South because of slavery, why did the North offer "freedom" to the slaves if they joined your Northern Union Army? Weren't the slaves already free where you lived up there in the north? I thought all this time that slaves were totally free of slavery in the North when the Civil War began? If they were free, then why did you "offer" the slaves living in the north, freedom if they joined the military? You mean when the Civil War began, all the slaves in the north were still slaves? And then, you Northerners "offered" freedom only if the slaves joined YOUR Union Army military? That's deep. So, the mystery of life is if you are needed to fight a war, it doesn't matter if you are black. But, when there is no war the black people and slaves become ignored and don't matter, as the political foot dragging culminated in a

Juneteenth celebration. America didn't particularly care if slavery continued, not even for 157 years after the Emancipation Proclamation was signed. And finally in 2021, driven by a boost of a much-needed popularity, an unpopular president signed the document into law as the other hand reaches beneath the table for another appeasing handful of crumbs for the Black people if Juneteenth didn't work. Because I do not have any respect for politicians, I do not care who the President was, but be sure that it was a signature of another political appeasement to control the masses by manipulation, and has absolutely nothing to do maintaining equality.

Research leaves one to wonder if we have learned anything about the dark side of our American history. Maybe it's time we began learning wars are fought over politics, power, money and greed. However, the "freedom" we are given could likely be a perception of deception as history proves otherwise. Very few countries are blessed with real freedom. Is the impending World Order going to allow exchange of mega assets to continue at the cost of more death to American citizens and massive destruction? It just seems we are in a world where one side is bad and the other side is equally as bad. Countries are headed to unite towards a One World Order. There will be a couple of countries that will not join the World Order and Taiwan is in China's sights and on the docket. The fight over possession of Taiwan will be the country that will most likely precipitate a WWIII. China wants Taiwan really bad, and the World Order cannot achieve its goal if it loses that precious commodity of Taiwan, even if it causes war and widespread killing of its people. In the meantime, the World Order will be gobbling up the riches of every other country it can. It brings to mind and I wonder if the war in Ukraine is just another systematic and programmed reset event and its people are victims, caught up in another process of taking or exchanging large valuable assets, all in the name of manipulative political order. Caught up in the middle of these mega "resets", the unarmed people suffer and die, when what all the people ever yearned for was to live in freedom, safety and without fear. Here in America, we are shamed by a history of 12 major wars since 1861. The Civil War killed 620,000 and do you American citizens remember who killed all those soldiers? Fellow Americans did. American citizens rose up against each other and killed each other over politically driven greed and monetary shifting of mega funds in the south, while politics threw in the carrot cake promise of abolishing slavery in America. Bullshit. And then, when the dust settled, slaves were still slaves and we all know prejudice will continue in perpetuity.

From the day America raised her flag to the present, we have been at WAR over 92% of the time. What is happening to this world and where are we headed? While the ever-expanding cosmos displays its grandeur in a universe of infinity, I can only wonder if there is still enough time to research the truth and know more about what is going to inevitably happen to American Citizens? I say there is time and the truth will set us free. Ask questions with those you know and trust. Look beyond some of their faults and you will see a person that has found true fulfilling joy in knowing that in spite of the worldly sins all of us struggle with every day and the morbid situation of food shortages, power shortages, gas price manipulation, wars and rumors of wars, God is still sitting on the Throne because He is the King of Kings and Lord of Lords!

josephusflaviussolo.com

FACTS TO RESEARCH: 1917 to 1923 = 26 racial massacres

1919 Red Summer and a plethora of racial prejudice against not just the black people, the brown people, the yellow, green and purple (even if some of those colors of people even existed, American prejudice would figure out a way to include them as second class citizens as well, without hesitation.)

The secret sterilization of Indian women in America up until 1980. So, the American doctors who worked for the government to secretly sterilize women failed miserably with their "Socratic Oath" and money was the driving force to do these things against America's people and nearly every doctor in America is driven by money.

Early America wouldn't allow blacks to read or vote for decades after they were granted freedom of slavery.

Japanese American Citizens were rounded up and forced to move to "camps" during WWII, because our political leaders felt the Japanese were a threat to America during the war. How utterly stupid. Imagine the political idiocy rounding up all of the German people in America during WWII, and forcing them in "camps" as well….so how come we didn't do that?

A 2015 Equal Justice Initiative Report has details about the 4,400 documented racial terror lynchings that occurred from 1877 to 1950. Singer, songwriter Lionel Richie was heard to say, "We don't have Justice, but we do have Just Us.

Chapter 30

1812, WAR WITH CANADA?

I suppose all of us have known that we fought a war against our more intellectual friends in the north? Well, when we declared war in 1812 on Great Britain again, some Easter Egg Brain at American Headquarters decided to declare war on Canada too, right? So, off we go, and over the northern border. When American military forces ran over to Canadian soil they were met with a voracious Indian and civilian fighting force. In the meantime, Canada and Great Britain's ships had complete control of the entire Atlantic Ocean, including all the way down the eastern coast of America. If that wasn't enough, British troops marched in to Washington, D.C. and burned down our Whitehouse – well I guess THAT got our attention Whoops. NOT!

In August 1812, Former President Thomas Jefferson, who had 600 slaves of his own, boasted to the editor of a Philadelphia newspaper "the acquisition of Canada... will be a mere matter of marching." Bull.

I am surprised Britain and Canada didn't continue their blockade of the entire eastern borders of America, and keep us completely devastated in our downward spiral towards national bankruptcy. America's Shipping

Industry turned upside down and we surrendered. After burning down the Whitehouse I remain surprised at why Great Britain didn't take back America.

So, the war just went away, and time marched forward. In fact, let's take a look at how many total wars America DID have since we declared our independence, and became this great nation for all the other countries look up to on this planet.

Total: 77 wars, or "conflicts", since 1776. And the beat goes on........

So, the knot-heads in Congress and the president and everyone else working there in D.C. ran like a pack of coyotes when the British Forces arrived at the Whitehouse with torches in their hands. All of our politicians ran and hid like a pack of terrified sheeples, they ran scared and whined until they found out the British Forces left and they could come back to work, but they didn't have a building that could survive their inflated egotistical pontifications. We managed to build another Whitehouse and of course, we paid for it. However, the citizens forgot to learn by their mistakes and apply an effective housecleaning program before Washington politicians started up again. Instead, it was business as usual and the same dirty trash went back to work to plot their next scheme of the largest proportions. These same irresponsible political wimps were the very morons who worked their schemes until they could manifest another war. This time the war was on us. It was between us, and all about US. Wow, was that Civil War a doozy or what? The same blatantly ignorant group of snollygosters, with the exact mentality of a common moron were the same politicians that decided we needed to go to war with our neighboring states and kill over 620,000 of each other. Someone tell me why these politicians were not standing at the front line when England burned the Whitehouse down? Where were they when we fought the other 77 wars? Stupid decisions cause arterial bleeding in our country and American citizens are still manipulated with band aids.

Where is our logic?

josephusflaviussolo@gmail.com

3 MUSKETEERS OF EVIL

Chapter 31

———✥———

ONLY ONE HERO

We all know the definition of the word hero has changed throughout time. One who is admired for great or brave acts or display of fine qualities? I want to camp on the words "great or brave acts or display of fine qualities." At my age I have a ton of heroes; so many I can't list them all. I have been thinking about that and decided I would express my thoughts and conclusions. Who is your hero? When I was a young man, my heroes were Willie Mays, Mohammed Ali, John Wayne, my Aunt Priscilla and a few others. Of course, my mom and dad were both heroes because they served in the military during WWII. After thinking about each and every one of all my heroes over all these years, I realized every "hero" fell miserably short of having those "brave acts or display of fine qualities" on a *sustained basis*. An example of my life at home was: "Dad, when you were my hero, you were a broken down drunk most of my life. Mom, you were my hero, but you molested me as a child, and *so did your stinking dad*." Oh, yes. Grandpa Heller molested nearly all of my cousins as well and the entire adult family ignored the crime and became "shocked" years later when us kids finally said something.

I dragged that dirty baggage of anger around with me for years until I realized I needed resolve. Forgiveness was of paramount importance. When I forgave my parents, their slate became as clean and white as snow. Only through the power of biblical forgiveness am I able to know my mom and dad as my heroes.

My parents fell miserably short of having those sustained brave acts or display of fine qualities. Wouldn't you agree that sometimes all heroes fall short of those qualities? Let's all work towards hero status; the kind of hero who is well respected, is good for his or her word and known for their honesty and shows respect towards others. Wouldn't it be great if your children knew you as their real hero in life, who staunchly set great examples and was always respectful, fair, honest and just?

josephusflaviussolo@gmail.com

Chapter 32

BUS RIDE TO NOWHERE

My life was ripped out from under me when my parents separated. I was 7 when I was told one-full minute full of emotional words expressing terror no child should ever have to endure, "I'm leaving your father." The news staggered my 7 year-old mind. Emotional darkness and anguish over a trauma of loss went shooting through every cell in my brain and body. For a young boy, I was an emotional wreck, screaming and crying over a confused event I didn't even understand, only to be physically dragged to a bus, completely scared and confused and planted in a seat next to my emotional wreck of a mother. As the bus rolled away, I still remember the flowing tears that robbed me of the clarity to see my dad just standing there, not knowing what to do next as his image got smaller and vanished. The Westside Lumber Corporation was on strike, the Tuolumne Lumber yard closed down, jobs were scarce, my parents were in debt, dad was a bar fly and a drunk, who never took the time to even play catch or attend one of my numerous baseball games, or give me much of the time of day, except to go fishing. But that man was the only person I knew as dad, and his life was coming to an end as a husband and father. Mom had finally had enough of his unemployment, drunken stupidity bullshit, and respect in our little home had taken an extended leave of absence. Love waned as the marriage drifted away and I was dropped off in front of a bunch of weird, long brown government buildings I was forced to call "home". Dilapidated crackerjack buildings were left over from WWII in a small town called Manteca. "Home" became a very tiny kitchen, a tiny front room, and one little bathroom – ok, maybe a total of 420 square feet at best.

I don't mean to portray my life was as bad as the coal miner's daughter, but living with walls that were paper-thin to amplify noise attributed to lots of disrupted sleep. My nights were consumed by a continuous banter of loud hacking and coughing all through the night from an old neighbor, who I was sure would soon die. Eventually, I grew accustomed to the cough, and finally I was able to convert the hacking cough into a musical concert each night, slowly lulling me to sleep. The nights and days went on and my emotional frailty was taking its toll, both mentally and physically. I prayed and cried at night for months, missing the only dad I ever knew. I vividly recall not seeing my dad's face for well beyond a year, as the months of a torn family went slowly drifting away into obscurity and insecurity. I was a mess and my 2 years of emotional anguish fostered more hypersensitivity. School pulled me away from the only family I had left in mom, and served as more of a separation and agony through each day being separated and without my "family." Mom got a very low paying job with the government at Sharpe's Army Depot, and I never saw her until 5:30 p.m. every day. Dinner was small, mom was drawn and tired, stressed and distressed every night. She suffered from a lot of depression. Every comfort and security felt in the word "family" was destroyed. I remained in the darkness of no information about my dad for 2 years. I missed him every day and every night I prayed and cried.

I was never told about the particulars, or what led to their separation. After those 2 years, a glorious day of fulfillment and happiness

3 MUSKETEERS OF EVIL

re-entered my life. Mom told me my dad was coming to Manteca to join us as a family again. The word "family" heard in my 9-year-old ears was an experience of abounding joy beyond comprehension and the emotion of that gladness remains utterly unexplainable to this day.

Let me continue so you can know some of my private baggage. Let's see, when I was 2 ½ years old, I was jerked off by my mother a few times. When she was in an angry rage, she once beat me with a large red patent leather belt that left large bruises on each side of my hips and stomach (8 years of age). My, dad was a broken down drunk, suffering from severe PTSD from WWII and my grandfather on mom's side was busy molesting me and the rest of my cousins and damned if you wouldn't know it – NOT ONE OF THE ADULTS KNEW ABOUT IT. He was an evil child predator. All of us young cousins knew he was, but all of the adults acted like they were aghast and in a complete state of shock and horror when they were told the truth 35 years later!" I say bullshit – they all knew something was wrong, but didn't do anything about it.

Comment: I am sure many of us have had a profound experience and memories that would make my problems look like a cakewalk. But, the preponderance of the question is: "Is Forgiveness a real possibility?"

Indeed. The Book I read tells me that to forgive means to forgive Biblically. Forgiveness is defined in Scripture as placing the offending person's sins as far away as East is to West, never to be brought up again. Not ever, or ever. If a person comes to you and asks for forgiveness, read, use and apply the scriptural instructions you will receive in the Word. I carry no baggage, anger or animosity for those I have forgiven. I see a lot of people, dragging their baggage behind for years and years and are still angered or troubled over past experiences. Forgiveness becomes a super-natural event once you are able to forgive, because it will give you peace beyond understanding. So, I guess the empirical question would be "if we are unable to forgive others of their sins, how can God ever "forgive" us of our sins?

I only wish I were able to reveal more about the word "forgiveness." As a dad, I once had to forgive a man who should have been dragged away to a field, castrated and left to die because of what he had done to one of my daughters. I had other variations of how I was going to deal with this man until God got in the way. I wish I could share the full story, but it's not possible. This monster did not ask me or my family for forgiveness, and the worm of hatred was slowly eating me up inside. Not long after I was able to Biblically forgive this monster, the coals were placed on his shoulders and he died from two back-to-back heart attacks, (probably just a coincidence, right?).

Chapter 33

VICTIM OF SESQUIPEDALIAN LOQUACIOUSNESS?

Meyers-Briggs Personality testing confirmed I love to talk, reason, learn and communicate in an INTJ world. I am an older gentleman, who has engaged in loquacious conversation with some of my friends and relatives and that's ok because I am, unfortunately. When I turned 18, I was given an opportunity to excel beyond my imagination. The things I've done, places I've gone and lifetime experiences were by no means average or dull. I didn't grow up in a small town and remain there all my life, living the boredom of not much to do and not caring to go anywhere until the end of life. Not me. I had an opportunity to join the U.S. Army or go to jail for 6 months and pay a stiff fine. I am glad I chose the Army. Life at home was an endless series of peaks and valleys of emotional unbalance and inconsistency. My home was saturated with alcohol, hatred, unforgiveness, molest, a small child's death combined with incessant arguing and upset. The thought of jail might have been a nice calm vacation away from my home, but I needed to get away longer, and do what I could to be smarter. That's why I chose the Army. Honestly, it was the only way to get rid of some bad friends, get away from my dysfunctional parents and fix stupid me, because I did not see any value added by becoming a loser with a police record; I knew I had to straighten up, real quick. After joining the Army, I realized it was the only fair and consistent mother and father I ever knew. The Army never changed the rules. Once you learned the rules, life was great in the military if you applied yourself and made use of your tour and didn't mind killing people. The only part of the Army I sought after was a professional skill and more education in a different kind of jail. (Army, lol)

And excel I did. I rapidly poured through every Army Tech Manual and studied regulations with a voracious appetite. I constantly asked questions and listened to every word, every process and every kind of program. I was taught and attended more military schools than most of the soldiers, and as long as the check was paid in full by my Uncle Sam, I would go. Uncle Sam paid for a ton of college courses at night. Some were during the day. I ended up becoming a helicopter pilot and test pilot and served in places like Germany, Ethiopia and Vietnam. At 21, I was teaching courses in military weaponry, teaching courses in helicopter maintenance, aircraft forms and records, and crew chief responsibilities. I also taught night high school courses for those in the military who did not graduate from high school. I had an audience of many troops and every one listened if they expected to pass the course and get their GED. At 23, I was serving a tour in Vietnam as a combat pilot and maintenance officer for the 57th Assault Helicopter Company in Pleiku, Vietnam. I was the night Maintenance Officer and Test Pilot in charge of the 2 maintenance crews, the inspectors, the crew chiefs and gunners and 26 Huey helicopters. Many nights I would be out test flying to insure the broken, battle scarred Huey would perform its combat mission the next day. I was given a hell of a lot of responsibility for the age of 23 and lives were at stake every single day that depended on my skill and abilities. I too, flew many of the countless combat day missions as well. Actually, my Maintenance

Officer duties at night were secondary to flying a combat mission every other day as I was expected to do. I don't even remember sleeping much during that year. I came back to the states and ended my career after serving 8 years. I was awarded the Bronze Star and Air Medals. When I got home, I got a job with the government, and held such positions as an Engineer in Electronics at McClellan AFB for a few years, then became a Quality Engineer at a major Rocket Motor Plant. Just so you know, some of the Space Defense Initiative technology is still in low earth orbit watching over the United States every day and night, assuring our safety in the event of a hostile nuclear attack. I was the guy who signed the DD form 250 that authorized payment of upwards of $238 million dollars worth of rocket motor. Over the years, my lone signature authorized payment of hundreds of millions of dollars worth of various rocket motors, etc., on behalf of the government. I had such government latitude I could comfortably speak with top civilian Aerospace Directors, Engineers specialized in most aircraft commodities and aerospace disciplines. Learning was easy for me. I listened. I rejected the upheaval of an inconsistent home life by redirecting negativity into talking and listening to others who had wisdom; always learning and listening. I must admit I did an awful lot of talking over the years, and those that listened to my instruction were students, troops, maintenance crews, fellow pilots, commanders, directors, supervisors, engineers and assembly workers specialized in numerous aircraft/aerospace fields. Most of the time I was asking questions to eagerly learn everything I could every day. In the aerospace industry, I had the authority to shut down a process, a building, all the maintenance workers, a rocket motor program, an F-22 process or the most advanced aircraft deployed Quickstrike mines. I have authored aircraft/engine Tech Manuals for the Army and was still eager to learn.

Then I retired. Retirement suddenly became the most boring event in my life. In 2003, the maintenance crews stopped calling for an upcoming inspection, Managers and Directors didn't need me anymore and managing government contracts were a thing of the past. My Level

II Radiographic Interpreter's license expired, my OSHA experience was no longer needed, STAT 1 statistical processing techniques and analysis was no longer needed, my certifications for welding, wiring, Magnaflux, ultrasound, dye penetrant, composites, Mil-Q, and ISO Standards examiner, Titan II and III and IV schooling, military and civilian college courses, degrees and government knowledge was no longer needed. No engineers came to my door asking me to authorize a repair on a rocket motor.

For the first time in my life, I was no longer needed for a mind as active as mine. For the first time in my life my intelligence, experience, authority, and keen ability to develop and achieve communicative skills, and not cause anyone to become intimidated, had waned. I treat everyone from a bum to a rocket scientist with utmost respect until I knew otherwise. In the aerospace industry I was well respected. I was always honest and fair, willing to discuss but not argue. I abhor those who, when angry, don't have enough decency to speak to the person in private and in a civil manner. Like a conniving snake was the person who waited until others were around to make a big show in front of other people. Do I believe in a good ass chewing? Yes and yes. I've deserved a lot of ass chewing – most times were in a private room or sequestered outside. Public admonishment and disrespect is when everyone else gets to listen as if to feed on the hearing of someone being corrected or disciplined. Think again about the word respect. But, if you have something to chew my ass about, let's not make a circus out of it. Ass chewing is between you and the ass you're going to chew. If you are not chewing that ass with respect, it's you that stands looking like an ass. Make it private, between you and the other person. If your anger is not righteous anger then show no anger at all. Handle it privately and be respective, and people will listen respectfully for your corrective criticism with absolute honesty. Heaven forbid, but if you happen to harbor something I have done and not reasoned with me it is clearly your fault for not coming to me. If not taken care of, the arrogance, ineptitude, greed, anger and animosity will consume you from within like a worm slowing eating you from the inside.

Besides, isn't that how wars start?

josephusflaviussolo@gmail.com

Chapter 34

───◆───

ETHIOPIAN BIBLE

I purchased this old bible at sort of an outdoor garage sale on a street corner in Addis Ababa, Ethiopia, Africa. If you were walking towards the U. S. Mapping Mission Headquarters, the blue house was down the road about a half mile at the next street corner. The blue house was well known as a cool bar, and full of the prettiest Ethiopian girl prostitutes in Africa, waiting to make a deal. I bought a bible from some old lady on a dusty street corner, located ½ mile away from our military quarters. She was bent over from the years of hard work, her hair was grey with eyes glazed over from a hard life, and walked with a slight limp. She appeared to be the age of 40. The Ethiopian people loved to barter prices and the display of items were laid onto blankets, so after a fair amount of bartering with her in her own language, the old lady was very happy to be paid the $2.00 U.S. money (5 dollars Ethi), that consummated the purchase.

This bible was a very rare book. It was handwritten by an old scribe in an ancient language known as Guz or Ehiopic. Its pages are vellum (skin from an animal). I have not counted the pages, but I would estimate this book has 200 pages. It is at least 1,000 years old, dating somewhere between the 7th and 10th century. The source I used was www.tertullian.org/fathers/harden_ ethiopic_literature.htm (an introduction to Ethiopic Christian Literature.)

The cover and back are made of wood. I would guess the wood to be a wood biblically described in the Bible as "Shittim wood", indicating the wood species to be an acacia. The front wooden cover was broken at one time and was repaired using some kind of animal gut thread. Also, there are a few pages of the vellum that were torn and sewn back using the same type of thread. The scripture is written in Black and Red colors on the vellum. Because it is hand scribed the book is one of a kind and was written well before the Gutenberg printed bible. The Gutenberg Bible was the earliest major book printed, using mass-produced movable metal type in Europe. While the Gutenberg Bible helped introduce printing to the West, the process was already well established in other parts of the world. The Chinese were pressing ink onto paper as early as the 2nd century A.D., and by the 800's they were producing full-length books using wooden block printing. The language used in the making of the Ethiopian Bible is an ancient language known as Gee'z, Guz, also translated as "Gi'iz", or referred to by some as Ethiopic, which is also an ancient Semitic language that originated in the northern region of ancient Ethiopia at that time known as "Cush".

Cush is now called Ethiopia, as we recall in ancient history, as the name of a region in Africa and its name is well documented in scriptures of the bible. Cush had a long history before the country was changed to the name Ethiopia. In the bible, Miriam was guilty of unrighteous anger towards her brother, Moses. Apparently, Moses wasn't seeking proper counsel and Miriam blamed his wife, and scornfully referred to Moses as being "married to that Cushite!" In fact, those were the scriptural words Miriam used. Miriam's slanderous accusations of disrespect for her brother Moses were heard by God and if you read the account in the Bible you will learn that as a result of Miriam's unrighteous anger,

God struck Miriam with Leprosy. Reading on, you will find that Moses asked God if He would not make her leprous. God replied because of the leprosy, she would remain outside of the tent city for 7 days for cleansing. At that period in history, anyone identified with leprosy was immediately cast out of the tent city. The Levitical Priests were appointed to verify if a person was cured of the disease and were the only ones authorized to admit the person back into the rest of the populous within the tent city. You might ask "why" were the Israelites living in a "tent city?" The history of the Bible indicates the Israelites were freed from the bondage of slavery in Egypt. As the Israelites wandered the desert for 40 years their city became a conglomerate of numerous tents that had some sort of a protective barrier around the outside perimeter. Anyone afflicted with the disease of leprosy was cast out of the tent city until such time they either died or were cured (of course, there was no cure – except the miraculous cure God gave to Miriam after she spent 7 days outside of the city as God mandated.) People wonder why God struck Miriam leprous? Was it because her Cushite skin color was BLACK! *I believe this to be the first documented biblical account of prejudice against a black woman.* I also believe that every black person on this earth should know that GOD was the very ONE that set mankind straight about black people and black people should rejoice and have the wisdom to know that God Himself, declared that jealous prejudice of Black People would not be tolerated. Praise God! I am constantly reminded that God personally intervened to punish Miriam for her anger and what she said. I understand this part of scripture as being; when God broke in on the earthly conversation of Miriam's anger towards Moses and punished her with leprosy. God has broken in on my conversations every time I've had something nasty to say about black people or any of God's people.

Has God spoken to you yet? I'm talking about all colors of skin. Are we willing to consider that God loves all of His creation? God doesn't see color. He sees inside your heart, and my heart was hardened negatively towards black, white, yellow, red and brown skin. I don't want to stand before the Judgement seat of Christ and have to suffer the public disgrace, torment and embarrassment of knowing I did not repent of such anger and disrespect I have had for black people, yellow people, brown people and red people, and even my own white people. I learned prejudice because I was taught prejudice. God's Word taught me how the intervention took place during Miriam's moment of anger and sinful expression of words towards Moses and his black Cushite (Ethiopian) wife.

Martin Luther King was scripturally correct when he said "God loves all of God's people." I confess the error of my ways. I will keep this biblical story much closer to my heart because "I am bound by the scripture and its teachings." I confess that I have not been tolerant of all colors of God's people.

If God is not the author of prejudice via bigotry, animosity, bias, injustice, hatred, intolerance, enmity, chauvinism and discrimination, who is the author and orchestrator? He will reveal his morbid intentions soon and most assuredly deceive the world and become leader of the World Order. The 3 Musketeers of Evil will be revealed.

josephusflaviussolo@gmail.com

Chapter 35

NEVER SCOLD A CHILD
W/O AGAPE

WE SHOULD NEVER SCOLD A CHILD to make them feel guilty. We should scold in a manner the child feels that he or she is letting you down. All children are created and endowed with a very powerful love known as "agape love." Every new born will anxiously give that precious agape love to you on the first day the baby hears or sees you mom, and you too, dad. So, here's the question. My tiny heart is just oozing everywhere with agape love, and when I share it with you, will you teach me how agape love works and what it means? Because I was told that once I freely give you my agape love, it could never be destroyed, it can never be voided, diluted, negated, cancelled or taken back. Agape Love is exempt of hatred because its in these times I know you accepted my outpouring agape love, and you will love me so indelibly, you could never possibly stop loving me any more than I could ever stop loving you. That's agape love. Agape love is indelible, and cannot be removed, abandoned, ignored, lost or discarded.

And, when you raise me up, teach me respect so I can show you respect in return. Mom, Dad, teach me patience and kindness so that I will learn by your example. Teach and show me things and take time to explain to me everything you know about nature and respect for others. Teach me honesty and I will learn the definition by your example. And please don't scream at me or ever induce guilt. I want to love and respect you so much that I will not feel guilty, but rather, hurt inside thinking I have let you down. So, be tender with me, teach me honesty and the meaning of the agape love you have for me. As I grow up, I will be looking for you to both to be my teacher, protector and provider and I am going to watch you very closely mom and dad, and learn all of the good things about you and look to you as my rock when I grow up because I am going to watch you both very closely and learn every bad thing you do, too. And, if your going to be a bad mom or dad, just know I loved you from the time I was growing in mom's tummy and my agape love for you is forever and ever no matter what. When I grow older and through the years I want you to reflect and find joy in the good things you taught me. Because Mom, Dad you were the ones setting the examples – right?????????

josephusflaviussolo@gmail.com

FACT: An adult will laugh an average of 4 times per day. A child will laugh an average of 150 times a day.

Chapter 36

───── ⚮ ─────

Am I going Crazy?

How many times have you heard the saying, "that person is out of their mind!" Have you ever wondered what might have prompted a Republican Senator to suddenly turn 180 degrees from his normal Republican responsibilities and shockingly vote "thumbs down" against President Trump's proposal, and defiantly vote "NO" in opposition against all of his fellow Republicans? That guy needed a brain scan. Oh, yes he did have a brain scan, and I can tell you many Americans had a strong reason to suspect that he was not of his "right mind". So, even after we knew he was dying of brain cancer, no one apparently cared enough to consider that his brain was riddled from a horrible disease and he might have been mentally unable to use common sense in the job of representing Republicans. Now does that seem possible? Is it also possible that Hitler, Stalin and people who do horrible things just might be out of their minds? Take a look at our Democratic hopeful, Mr. Biden, who introduces his wife as his sister, forgets what he's saying and replies with blathering words that make no sense. That fellow might need a brain scan also. Think about it. This message is not to condemn these people who are out of their minds – it could very well be a medical issue and not a political issue. Oh, by the way, you folks that support our recent violence, theft, burning, killing and defiance of law; you should be getting a brain scan too. Do we Americans have any idea how many lives have been lost, or monetary gain has been attributed to people making crazy decisions? We will continue to suffer with the hidden realm and possibility of insanity. A simple brain scan should be required for each and every person who holds any position of AUTHORITY. WWII cost us countless billions of dollars and a lot of lives were lost on both sides. Someday, intelligence will tear aside the veil of ignorance.

For I am certain, that when Democracy fails in America, all other countries will collapse and implode, and be drawn towards the black hole of widespread Un-Americanism, terrorism, prejudice, killing and hatred. The only proof left that we existed on this earth at all will be smothered in the remaining dead bodies and our last fingernail marks holding on to life in desperation, while being dragged screaming and crying towards the inevitable black hole of death. Again, my fellow Americans, our blood and dead bodies will be the only remaining evidence that humans existed at all. I only ask that you diligently, carefully and intelligently keep apprised of the attitude, motivation and hatred that is raging across American soil today and keep an open mind that dark empath politicians are manipulating the way we think. I can only pray we don't ignorantly align ourselves in a lock step towards the black hole of World Order. It seems that is the direction we are going so I'm going to keep my nails filed down to the nub so I don't leave any telltale tale nail marks as we all become drawn towards the black hole of lawlessness, disorder and hatred. God gave us a brain filled with love, compassion, respect, forgiveness, responsibility, logic and truth – so, keep these things in mind as the son of perdition dances with his fiddle of evil, eternal darkness, damnation and deceit. The 3 Musketeers of Evil are waiting in the shadows.

josephusflaviussolo@gmail.com

Chapter 37

HERE IS A SECRET RESOLVE FOR THE WIFE WHO IS STRUGGLING WITH THE HUSBAND

On a golf course years ago, a friend was complaining about his wife. He said she walks around grumpy most of the day and seems upset about something and says she "doesn't even know where to start………….." With beautiful blue skies, great fairways and greens, the rest of the golfing day was uplifting and I let him win the round, but I couldn't get off the words, "she doesn't even know where to start." I thought because he was many years older, older couples had nothing to say to one another. I wondered why? My curiosity revealed an astonishing dream.

In the dream, I wanted all women of this land to focus on the jobs around the house that you ladies do that **husbands "feel they should NOT have to do."**

Like: Clean up the house, clean the bathrooms, sweep and mop the floors, wash the windows, go get groceries, make the beds, do the

dishes, water lawns and flowers, take the kids to school, cook all break-
fast, lunch and dinners, vacuum, wash, dry and fold all the clothes,
iron, take the animals and the family to the doctor, feed the cat, groom
the dog and worry like hell your children are safe in school, and worry
that something dreadful doesn't happen to your husband at work such
as a policeman or a helicopter pilot in the Army, then fall into bed
late at night and pray. Apparently, it was me, who became motivated
to help the little lady out around the house only when I wanted some
loving.

The dream went on as I realized I had been a stupid man for years.
So did my wife. She knew the true meaning of "help mate" by carrying
my load each and every day. Oh yeah you say, "I work." Really? Spend
a day with her and take on some of the load around the house. I felt
the guilt of falling short of the load I should help carry and perform
some of her duties and help lighten her load. If so, I dreamt I could
lose some weight off of that lazy ass of mine. In fact, it was a terrible
dream because she stopped talking to me, got crabby and cut me off
for not helping out around the house enough! She used THE SECRET
WEAPON AND MADE IT NUCLEAR!!!!!!!!!!!!!!!!! And then my wife
ran out into the street and yelled to a large group of people "HURRAY
for wives everywhere!!"

When I woke up, I felt so guilty I took the garbage out for her (lol).

The truth is I needed a better understanding of the importance of
loving, caring and volunteering for some of the daily house jobs and
display more of a willingness to help my wife out with her daily duties.

For all the helpmates, who continue to do everything around the
house and have no idea how you could explain this dilemma to your
husband, I can only wish they would have the same dream too. You
might write your man a love letter and ask him to be a proactive help
mate and share in some of the house duties. It's the best anti-crab medi-
cation I can think of.

SIGNED: John. The former stupid man, who is trying his best to be a loving and kind helpmate, who is willing to help bear the load. I like the story of the two married women sitting together having coffee, when one asked, "Why don't marriages swap poles like the Sun does every 11 years?" "How about if we change the way of doing things and give men and husbands the right to run the country and the home for 11 years. Then, we "swap poles" and let us women run this country and the house for 11 years!" Imagine, safer schools, balanced budget, flat tax system, no wars, no civil war, proactive medical plan that applies to ALL American Citizens and not just the "select political group", abolish prejudice and crime, etc., (as the hypothetical list goes on and on).

josephusflaviussolo@gmail.com

Chapter 38

---

73 TRILLION CELLS

If you were given a billion dollars (1,000,000,000), each year, you would have to live for 10 centuries to receive one trillion dollars (1,000,000,000,000,000).

If you have been extremely healthy all of your life you've done a great job with your diet and I would like to know your secret. The average human body is comprised of 73 or so trillion cells. That is a million billion 73 times. 73 trillion cells and we only need the ONE bad cell in the body to spoil an afternoon's destiny. Research of the poultry and beef industry reveals a shocking revelation, that apparently humans feel they don't need, and it all has to do with maximizing levels of vitamins and minerals. Researchers found that when chickens were deprived of certain vitamins and minerals, the chickens would become frail, sit back on their haunches and look straight up, lose feathers, couldn't walk, go blind, and the list goes on. However, the Poultry and Beef Industry got smart after their research and found that if every chicken and cow was fed a diet that maintains the maximum vitamin and mineral levels, the beef and chicken industry would produce a fat healthy chicken and a beefed up beef.

Now that we all understand how the Poultry and Beef Industry maintains their productivity through maximizing V&M levels, what has the Human Industry done for us humans and our 73 trillion cells? Yet, we continue to suffer from a host of afflictions and die from a plethora of known and unknown diseases. Somebody needs to start tracking our personal vitamin and mineral levels.

FACTOID: The "Human Industry" doesn't care about the health of our 73 trillion cells. I suspect most humans have never read the health chart deficiencies directly attributed to inefficient vitamin and mineral intake. So, why and how is our health less valuable than a chicken or a cow? If the Poultry and Beef Industry figured out how to optimize the health and immunity of a chicken or a cow, how come no one is following our personal vitamin and mineral levels so that we humans can live long and stay healthy? There is much money to be made using reactive medical procedures as opposed to proactive medical procedures. It comes in the form of a band aid or "so, let's give this other expensive pharmaceutical drug a try and we'll see you again in 3 weeks." Most doctors are focused on waiting until the patient comes in with a problem or sickness. Proactive health measures are the key to prevention. The Medical Health Industry does perform some proactive health measures but vitamin and mineral levels that will boost the Immune System are ignored. The Health Industry does not provide us with a routine lab report that documents historical data to track our total vitamin or mineral levels, so nobody knows and nobody cares. So goes any interest in boosting or maximizing our Immunity System.

Most medical students receive an average of a whopping 19 hours of nutrition courses during med school. It's no wonder doctors will tell us to "just take a good multivitamin each day and you'll be fine." Really? So, does the doctor know your personal zinc, potassium, selenium, cobalt, copper, B1, B6, B3, manganese and magnesium levels?

While I am well aware that some vitamins and minerals are included in the doctor ordered routine blood tests, patients do not know all of their V&M levels and doctors don't either. Deficiency of only one vitamin or mineral can have detrimental health effects. Who has their Vitamin and Mineral levels checked every six months or at least once a year? When was the last time you heard of a doctor requesting a complete vitamin and mineral check for any affliction? Still make you wonder? It's called Profit and Greed and all one needs to do is "follow the money and follow the motive for the money."

I am beginning to think of the stiff necked doctors who didn't believe washing of hands was of any importance at all when it came to disease and transference of germs during the Civil War. Some historians say as many as 700,000 soldiers died due to bacteria and disease from the unwashed hands of a doctor.

josephusflaviussolo@gmail.com

Chapter 39

———— ∞ ————

RETIRED OF BEING NICE

I am Retired of being nice. Oh, I was a proud American Color of a man up until I turned 72 years of age. Then, I decided to retire and pass the torch to the next generation of Americans who would be willing to die in combat for this country here in America, and not hesitate to help a soldier in combat NO Matter What His or Her Color is! Well, when I reached out to pass the torch of being fair and impartial no one was there. However, prejudice in America abounds like fleas on a dog.

If I ever sat in a foxhole with you, you can be damn well assured I got your back. I don't care what color you are. Flying Hueys in Vietnam during 71-72, with mini-gun barrels that sizzled in the rain and 2.75 rockets launched to stave off the enemy just long enough to get a Medi-Vac into your LZ and fly you to the nearest hospital; all of us in the helicopter knew you as a fellow soldier. A soldier in combat depends on survival and has nothing to do with color. We knew each other as brothers in a hostile country, but when we all got back home to our safe country, hostility towards color raised its ugly head again.

Army hospital staff and patients didn't have time to think about color. Survival was of tantamount importance. I crashed a Huey in II Corps after being mortared out of the sky during take off out of Fire-base 42, 13 days before my tour of duty was over. Dust and dirt went everywhere when we hit the ground, while my fellow combat brothers of all colors shot back at the enemy we fought our way to safety of an armored personnel carrier. In Vietnam, I never thought about color nor did anyone else. Being a soldier in battle is where you see real brotherhood. What has happened to us? Why are we so caught up in our animosity and "hatred of colors?" We have all failed miserably in the eyes of God. This is not a sermon. It's a Wake-Up Call for all of us colors of people.

Only 1 enemy hypersonic warhead needs to break through our U.S. atmospheric defense system and ALL electrical power will cease to exist in America. I know SDI, and I am talking POWER OUTAGES for long extended periods of time. Widespread killings will occur in our attempt to survive in our perplexing new environment of winter darkness and terror. Murder will prolifically abound under the world of darkness each night and fear will strike us all while holding our families in our foxhole homes of useless protection and be rendered powerless against a civil war separated by color and prejudice. More importantly, we need to set aside color and work together to survive if such a disaster were to take place. Instead, we could fight each other, kill, rape, steal each others food supplies and I am sure panic and fear will reign as the devil dances to the fiddle of eternal death. When America turns upside down, our survival will depend upon whether we kill each other to survive or work together towards a common cause like peace, before a scenario like this enters our manipulated minds. We had a close brotherhood in Vietnam and I can only pray we aren't thrown to the side of a curb and left on our own to survive. Let's come together and build a big foxhole and fight the devil together. Pandemonium and panic of the masses could suddenly affect all of us with even more murder, plunder, and terrorism in America where widespread rape will become a nightly occurrence. Now, brother............ are you ready to call me brother? Survival will depend upon all of you colors of humanity. I pray you are, so you better know me as brother when you jump into my foxhole.

When I returned home from Vietnam, I lost many brothers of color. After Vietnam was over, I guess us colors of others didn't need each other any more. After I got back home to America, I learned how to be prejudice, and yes, I was right out in the street of my mind fighting against your color as you fought back. I continued fighting the battle of skin color for 58 years and learned to be prejudice real good. What a dirty rag of animosity and bigotry I coveted towards people of all kinds and all races. I am not proud of this and I have the promise of resolve.

This old soldier made a final decision about the human race and our different colors of skin. I am bound by the word of God to obey His Wisdom and on this day, I will stop all animosity, attitude, anger and negative expression towards all of God's people and work at showing love and respect for all people of every color. Skin color didn't matter on the battlefield or in the air and that's how I want to live my life every day, right here on this blessed earth until I catch a Huey ride to heaven. Some day mankind will understand we all share DNA from a Godly source, fake science refuses to consider. We are all brothers and sisters – why do we display such disdain and contempt towards one another? I want to hear from you.

Signed: A Combat Soldier of no color, RA1890ETHI
            United States Army

In memory of my father, who valiantly served in combat during WWII, 394060—(HMS troop ship Rhona survivor).

In memory of my mother, who served in the U.S. Navy during WWII.

josephusflaviussolo@gmail.com

Chapter 40

UFO's, Who Is In Charge?

Flee in fear of the flying machine, as it dances in colors in an array of dreams; only begotten by serene exultations of mannerisms, and schemes of those in the flying machines. Up in the sky so wondrously high, fly up into the sky of divine; where time may not find the time for a world so designed with its mansions so near, can't be touched or smitten by fear, up and up to the sky so high that infinity intersects with God's infinity of divinity high, forever and forever and ever. Selah   (a poem by J. Flavius Solo)

Mironite (as described by Phil Schneider), is a substance that is described as a "hard rubberized metallic slag" that burns off during very high velocity. Is that why sparks or erupting slag particles are seen shooting off the sides of UFO's in flight? Is it possible that Mironite could be the material being used as a surface cooling couplant for the unidentified flying objects we chase and cannot catch with our fastest warplanes? America has cooled leading surfaces of missiles in the past to counteract extreme surface temperatures. The only reason accuracy is sustained at speeds of 260,000 mph, is because of a liquid couplant extrusion process to keep leading edge surfaces cool, thereby eliminating the problem of heat distortion and diminishing target accuracy. The Transpiration Cooled Nose Tip (TCNT) exudes a liquid alcohol mixture to cool the nose tip during flight of the High Endoatmospheric Destructive Interceptor (HEDI) missile designed for the Space Defense Initiative (SDI). A plethora of unidentified objects have been seen in hyper-speed flight for hundreds of years by us earth dwellers. I believe the only time our eyes ever witness seeing a genuine UFO is because the craft has slowed to speeds lower than 38,000 miles per hour so that it can be seen with the naked eye. For example, it is said a TR-3b Black Mantra can reach speeds of 42,000 mph. If this craft were flying at 2,000' AGL, would anyone see it in the air traveling speeds above 38,000 mph? Not likely. You wouldn't even see it in space at such speeds.

Light travels at 669 million miles per hour. What if terrestrial or extraterrestrial vehicles "slow down" long enough to recharge their magnetic energy sources? I feel that such vehicles exist and do slow down to human viewing speeds from time to time to recharge their system or to make sharp maneuvers, then accelerate to velocities we cannot see with our naked eye. I believe it is at such times we are able to see them in flight at lower velocities. Of course, it is well understood that other sightings go beyond a recharge or slowing speeds for the human eye to follow due to the fact that history has recorded a plethora of visitations from an array of different shape, sizes and appearance of these aliens and their craft capable of fantastical maneuvers and phenomenal sighting/visitations. So, the intrinsic question is who are they? If Russia or China has UFO technology it would seem they would have used their capability as a weapon and taken over the world long ago. Is it also likely that if America had this technology and capability we would have no more wars on this planet? It seems extremely possible aliens could rule over this earth very easily with their technologically advanced spacecraft. Why have they not done this is anyone's guess. What if there are different dimensions of time located right here on this planet and aliens are not authorized to intrude, assist or alter our dimension and technology in any way? If that were the case, what is the reason for the numerous sightings of UFO's we've seen since we bombed Japan using nuclear warfare? Someone or some thing is monitoring our nuclear launch facilities. UFO visitations have been witnessed at nuclear launch facilities in all countries. Each nuclear launch facility visited by alien forces causes pandemonium when all launch capabilities are compromised and shut down. One instance at a Russian launch facility caused all of the missiles to go green, indicating a potential launch. The Russians freaked out and went into a panic situation. Then, as quickly as systems went green, the activation process was shut down and the UFO left the scene. So, if this alien entity can control all nuclear launch facilities, what are the aliens waiting for? Why don't they just land and assimilate with humans? Over the history of mankind there are too many instances where ancient religious paintings depicted saucers and little beings sitting at the controls. What is the mystery? Have we had an alien presence since the Garden of Eden? If God rules over this world and an Evil entity exists in this world and is allowed to manifest all kinds of evil, who is God's enemy? Why are we witnessing these miraculous events? Are God's angels capable of a highly technological advancement, so futuristic these appearances are common in the spirit world? Are angelic beings capable of advanced flight? If so, one would have to consider there is a potential for the presence of evil that may have the same abilities. Who or what will remain a mystery until the right time comes for the truth to be revealed. While no one can rule out the possibility of the existence of extraterrestrials, terrestrials, aliens, Nordics, Grays, and little green men, one must consider who controls good and evil. The Bible is a book of value that gives peace in this lost world. There are several instances that record future events and it seems no one is looking in the right places. Instead, we spend billions of dollars for a telescope to see out into the past billions of years looking for answers that have been already given to us in a manual of life called the Bible. If science truly wants to do something of value let science dispute biblical scripture. Science is afraid to reason the factors of good and evil and investigate the profound historicity, geographical and prophetical accuracy contained in the Bible. While science is so quick to offer hypothetical reasoning there is no room to contemplate a spiritual realm exists and in that realm the spirit of good and evil is such that "men's hearts would fail." The 3 Musketeers of Evil will continue its mission of perdition.

FACTIOD: Travelling at 60,000 km per second, it would take 20 years to get to the nearest star.

FACTOID: China has 124 missiles in Low Earth Orbit (LEO). That's the same orbit as our International Space Station. Who are the missiles for?

FACTOID: Did you know if you walk to the moon it's about 240,000 miles away from earth. If a person fast walked an average of 9 miles a day it would take 70 years to get there. But, if a person ran 20 miles each day it would only take 8 years to get there. And, if you ran for 12,000 hours straight, you'd be sipping cold beer and Shirley Temples on the moon.

josephusflaviussolo@gmail.com

Chapter 41

THE DEVIL'S HYPOTHETICAL HYPO-PATHETICS

I am going to present to you a very hypothetical and situational future for America and the world. By no means am I rigid in my opinions regarding future events, nor am I an accomplished remote viewer. This hypothetical scenario of hypotheses are open for hypothetical disputes that readers may have regarding the following hypothetical possibilities and will remain as an uneducated guess. Some of this hypothetical content is immersed in truth, so read on.

An "interdimensional" is an entity who has mastered time travel and is as capable of leaving the physical body and transforming into a spiritual body. Many examples are recorded in the Bible. How about Evil and Good? We all have examples in our minds as to what is good and what is evil. Darkness simply proves it cannot exist where there is light because it flees from a room when the light comes on. However, when the light goes off, guess who is right there making a comeback to fill the room again with darkness. If we believe evil flourishes on this planet, who is the master?

Is it possible that Satan is the Supreme Interdimensional Commander of all of the alien species that are using UFO's as a means of travel? Some earthly news reviews state there may be over 46 different kinds of aliens, but I can't help thinking that all of the "other species" of aliens just might be one and the same. Witness accounts state that some of the other species of aliens are described as nice, helpful and sincere, while others have a foul and horrid smell and could be terribly evil. It could be possible the several different species of aliens are by design: To confuse and manipulate humanity.

In fact, many earthlings have encountered all variations of ET species, yet I believe there is only one Commander and Chief of evil reigning as supreme in the spirit world and he is known as Satan, who has absolute power and dominion over all the demons. They are the 3 Musketeers of Evil. Here is the most accurate description of the Godly living creatures that surround God's Throne in Ezekiel Ch. 37 as the author describes he was taken to heaven and saw a creature with wings and wheels within a wheel and used his limited ancient vocabulary to describe something quite celestial and technologically advanced. Satan's demons are described in the Book of Revelation Chapter 9. The question might remain as what are the aliens and who are the aliens? That is the great mystery. The empirical question is "what do the aliens want from us?" I try hard to see both sides of the dilemma of who they are and where they came from or what they want. But I can think of one scenario that generally makes sense to me. Were the thousands of mysterious cattle mutilations in America used as part of an investigation conducted by these demons to "create" their own kind of human species? Is it true that many human women have been abducted and used for Satan's creation? Are these aliens coming from another planet or distant galaxy and have they been here since the millennia of time? I believe we have had a number of angelic visitations, both consisting of the presence of good and evil. However, if we consider "angelic" beings as existing in our world the Book of Hebrews clearly states in the Bible: "Be not forgetful to entertain strangers: for thereby some have entertained angels unawares" KJV Hebrews 13:2. In our lifetime could you and I have entertained angels unaware? Billions of human souls have evidenced this "stranger" occasion and know it is something God has done for them, yet while the skeptics and disbelievers might be willing to agree something miraculous like that happened to them or someone they know about a Godly event or miracle, many still are reticent to the fact if there is a God, there also has to be the existence of Evil. Satan is his name. The Spirit of Evil is so obviously seen in today's world it seems incredibly beyond belief. Yet, many refuse to believe. At the battle of Armageddon, Satan will be the commander supreme as he stands with his demons and fellow human lost souls who were duped into believing in him. I can only hope his lost human souls will be few.

Elon Musk suggested during an interview "either there are a lot of aliens or no aliens." I would agree. I believe it may be possible several alien species could have visited this planet. I am intrinsically concerned about 1 of those species, because this species is in the business of attempting creation and taking over the world and taking down God's people. Who was the one that told God he could "create?" Scripture tells about some angels who abandoned their first estate and looked down upon the daughters of men. So, maybe Satan commanded his demons to possess a men who raped God's women and became the fallen angels who became demons? There is reason to suggest that the giant Nephilim were the product of demonic supernatural fathers, fallen angels (demons) and raped human women (Genesis 6:4 and Numbers 13:33). Jude 1:6 records that angels "kept not their first estate, but left their own habitation", He, (God) has reserved in chains those demons, who lost their first estate under darkness and were placed in the bottomless pit. What is the reason that demons could have possessed men who raped human women? Satan has always wanted to create and still does. Well, something big did happen in scripture for God to order a number of demons to be locked in the bottomless pit. That becomes a very deep and terrifying subject as you read where the bottomless pit is opened at a future time, because things on earth are going to get really nasty when that occurs. I abhor the thought. Well, so much for what the Bible has to say. Suffice it to say there may be a technologically advanced entity, capable of flying unidentified objects just as easily as understanding aliens could be from a different dimension of time, extraterrestrial or terrestrial. In any case, applying the knowledge of scripture in a cosmic environment, one does have to agree the scriptures are becoming more and more interesting as the biblical prophesies unveil and the world unfolds its destiny of evil as it begins to intensify in its revelation of finite purpose. I find it very interesting the aliens are not interested in communicating with people and seem much more interested in secret communications with only a "select" few. What could be the purpose for an alien's desire to share advanced technology with the strongest military force on earth for any reason other than evil? At present, an entity exists and is more than happy to influence the world's top political leaders and arm a potentially lethal military industrial complex with space technology that would dazzle Tesla's mind. Is our military industrial complex now equipped with such advanced ET technology it would astound and confuse the masses of humanity? How do we explain an alien presence has been known to visit the world's various military nuclear launching facilities in their flying saucers and demonstrate absolute authority by shutting down all nuclear missile launch capabilities? Why did alien visitation increase when the atom bombs were dropped in Japan and more atom/hydrogen bombs were tested by several countries? Could it be that mankind on this earth is acting like a loose cannon aboard ship, bent on self-destruction? Are good angelic aliens here to stop destruction of this earth? Could mankind's destruction of human life on earth in a nuclear holocaust adversely affect the normalcy of our galaxies' existence by initiating a celestial imbalance in the cosmos? Maybe. I would be more inclined to postulate there may be only two different alien entities, and that one of those entities is the existence of a Satanic false trinity and his demons. While earthlings agree some aliens purportedly seemed friendly, others are known as evil. What if nearly all of those 46 species of aliens are, in fact, demons?

3 MUSKETEERS OF EVIL

If that is so, then we have to consider how important and valuable our souls are because that's what it's all about.

If the earth's population is eliminated in a nuclear holocaust, is there possibly an angelic entity of alien who will intervene and not allow a destructive nuclear holocaust? It is very possible. Some one or some thing wants to control mankind. Satan has always been in the business of harvesting souls like a talent scout always on the lookout for humans who fail to recognize and reject the God of Israel. If man were to destroy mankind in a nuclear holocaust, Satan will not have an opportunity to control the earth and harvest all the souls he has in mind. Or if God exists, could His angels have been the ones demonstrating to the world's military how adept and capable they are with "shutting down nuclear launch sites?" It appears destruction by nuclear warheads is NOT on the slate of future events. In the meantime, Satan wants all of the souls of the creation of God he can persuade to join his side. He will need those "souls" to fight God at The Battle of Armageddon. Satan has always wanted to reign supreme and be god, just like he boasted in the presence of the true God of the universe. When Satan finished bragging about what he could do in the presence of God the evil one "fell like lightning from heaven." When he left, he took 1/3rd of the angels with him and they joined forces with Satan and became known as demons. My express intent here is not to scare anyone, nor is my motive to convert anyone, but let's reason together because my hypothetical take of our future existence may certainly have credence enough to persuade maybe at least 1 reader to research what the prophets have to say in the scriptures in an effort to know the truth about the things to come.

Is it about A Final War?

Sometime after WWII, a U.S a vital crypto communications entity quietly resided in Ethiopia, Africa. During WWII, Field Marshal Erwin Rommel's Nazi tanks raised hell with the Italians in Ethiopia for months before General Montgomery and his Sherman Tanks arrived at El Alamein and ran all the Nazi German forces out of the country.

Accurate maps of Ethiopia were a rarity until the military industrial complex realized one of the next wars would occur in the Middle East. The secret site in the northern region of Ethiopia was known as Kagnew Station, and was populated with agents of the Army Security Agency (ASA), Central Intelligence Agency (CIA), the Army Security Agency (ASA), the U.S. Strategic Communications Command (STRATCOM, the Navy Communications Command (NAVCOMM), and a signal research unit. Very few people knew of its real mission. Instead, the U.S. called it Kagnew Station. While the world was told Kagnew Station was "a telephone relay station and a deep space research project" the complex secretly served as center for the North American Aerospace Defense Command, now known as the Cheyenne Mountain Complex Space Force Station. My best guess is that someone in the military industrial complex thought to research the Bible to know there will be a future war in the Middle East (I can only wonder if soldiers of the military industrial complex realize the war in the Middle East is clearly described in scripture and prophecies as being the "FINAL" war). The military industrial complex knew Ethiopia's strategic geographical importance and we needed an accurate map of Ethiopia. Hence, the Ethi-U.S. Mapping Mission came into being. I spent 1967 and 1968 serving in Ethiopia. Two years of the most glorious time of my life. Ethiopia has so much biblical and archeological history it's mind-boggling! What a great tour of duty. The Ethiopian people were fantastic human beings and poor as could be. While the country toiled for food, Emperor Haile Selassie was its leader and from 1270 to 1975 he became the last of the Kings of the Solomonic Dynasty. So, the King's flag no longer displayed its Lion of Judah and the citizens are now living in a country that mandates State Atheism and is ruled by a Unitary Marxist-Leninist one party socialist republic. The people of Ethiopia are still as poor as they were 50 years ago and as they were over 2,000 years ago. If you do a research of Ethiopia, be sure to follow the money because the people are still under bondage and terribly poor where pestilence, death and hunger persists.

The present world is in a turmoil, confused by fake media and politics. Russia may start war with America and China may cause war over Taiwan. There is also a final war headed our way. It will begin with a 7-year peace treaty in the Middle East between the nation of Israel and the surrounding Arab nations. All will be wonderful for the first 3 ½ years. Peace will abound and the nation of Israel will live in true peace with security until the new Temple is built and the false christ, known as the anti-christ, walks in to announce he is the Messiah and the God of Israel. When you're cell phones tell you the Israeli people are suddenly fleeing to the hills of Petra in nearby Jordan, it's time to dig a deep foxhole and read the Book of John to learn about the Messiah who came to this world to save all His people. Yet, the world rejects Jesus Christ, the Messiah as readily as is seen in today's world. Some may feel the need to read quickly, who knows we may not have enough time to accept the free gift of grace and eternal life and believe that Jesus died for all of the sins of the world (and includes your sins hidden in a foxhole of life where ever you might be right now.) The World Order is quickly approaching. There will be wars and rumors of wars. Crime will run rampant, money and food will get scarce, prices for food and services will soar beyond comprehension, and there may be a civil war of prejudice and widespread killing could occur just to survive in a panicked world. We could all become as poor as the people of Ethiopia and American values could collapse causing a time of evil and uncertainty combined with mass hysteria. Possibly once again, American Citizens will be faced with a North/South enemy of racial prejudice to kill again in the name of survival just like the Civil War accomplished. It sounds very dark and bleak and I apologize for writing these things. I once read where 97% of the New Testament prophesies and 95% of the Old Testament prophecies have already been fulfilled. Each of those fulfilled prophesies have been 100% accurate, 100% of the time historically, scientifically and geographically. The remaining 3% and 5% prophecies are yet to come with an unveiling of such terror and panic it will make the evils of Nazi Germany and all of the past wars on this planet seem like a proverbial cakewalk in comparison. I feel there is a sudden movement of the spirit of God for citizens to come together and find the peace that God's truth gives. A widespread coming together of Christian citizens with the likes I have not seen before are also searching for the truth in an uncertain world. Friends come to me asking what might be going on in this new and changing fake informational unbalanced world. It seems people everywhere are looking for a shred of truth and are becoming concerned, while some are worried about what the future of mankind may reveal. God tells us to not worry and let worry, worry for its self. Personally, I am finding it harder not to consider the definition of the term worry. Soon there will be no more lemons to make lemonade and it will be a time to begin thinking about a cosmic God who created us in His image just so we could love Him back, in and for eternity. If those who disbelieve I would recommend you worry.

I want to share a hypothetical future of events with you. Imagine, there was a time in this world, where 1 man nearly conquered the entire world. Hitler and his Nazi armies were so deeply submerged in the occult there could have been one powerful fallen angel listening in on the future of our existence. Is it possible that technology of the "foo" fighters (UFO's) seen by pilots during WWII, were Satan and his Demons showing us fantastic sights in the heavens that may have included sharing such advanced technology with Hitler with a motive of eagerness to help Hitler win his war to become victorious and rule the world? Could part of Satan's plan include the sharing of an extraordinary technology only Germany would possess? Was Satan eager to share such futuristic technology with Germany so he and Hitler could usher in the new world order? Satan cannot see the future, but he could have been sure that Hitler would win the war and reign supreme. There is a conspiracy story that claims Hitler and the Nazis had a secret anti-gravity UFO called Die Glocke (the Bell) and the U.S. took possession of it after the war. Another conspiracy story suggests Germany was making "wonder weapons" including reports of a time machine.

Because Satan is incapable of seeing future events, he was more than willing to share some extremely advanced secret technology that Admiral Byrd stated to the Chilean Press. "We encountered a new enemy that could fly from pole to pole at incredible speeds." What if the Nazis were in on the plot when Satan and his UFO's left Germany and fled to the South Pole to reorganize and plan the next world order scenario of events? The Nazi Axis Forces were defeated and while most Nazis fled to South America, Satan and his demonic forces made their way to secretly dwell in the caverns of the South Pole? It would make sense if Satan fled from Hitler's presence and established his new headquarters in a land far way. Satan left Hitler's defeated Armies and dropped him like a dirty dishrag. Is it possible Satan could not ignore there was a stronger force present on earth and recognized earth's new and commanding world leader, 5 star General Dwight D. Eisenhower as the Supreme Allied Commander of the Allied Expeditionary Force of all of Europe? Satan knew that it was General Eisenhower, who made the decision to use the first atomic bomb and not Truman. Did Satan and his forces plot and patiently wait in the darkness to meet this new American conquering General of the world? History tells us that after WWII, as the allied victory was celebrated there was some unfinished military war business going on down at the South Pole. After WWII, the American military was certain an element of the Nazi regime was living in security at the South Pole. So, in 1946, the U.S. Navy established "Operation Highjump", known as Task Force 68 with a military force of 4,700 personnel, one of our largest aircraft carriers and a plethora of other various naval ships and aircraft to seek out and "destroy a hidden Nazi base." The "war" lasted 8 weeks with heavy casualty reports of American forces and sinking of ships who came against an incredibly advanced force that our military could not even begin to defend. Rumors and testimony was denied even though radioman John Szehwach stationed on the USS Brownson gave testimony about "UFO's flying out of the depths of the ocean", while pilot Lieutenant John Sayerson stated the "thing shot up vertically out of the ocean at such tremendous speed it was as though it were pursued by the devil."

The U.S. Navy limped home in defeat and placed a worldwide hush on the event, never willing to engage this technologically advanced enemy/entity again. An easy research of "Operation Highjump" will leave readers of this article to begin questioning exactly what the mission entailed. Contrary to what our government may reveal about such events, something very strange and aggressively evil met Admiral Byrd and his military forces when they arrived at the South Pole, a force of which was beyond our technological capabilities.

In 1947, there was a UFO crash in Roswell, NM. Who were these aliens? Is it possible there might be another civilization in another dimension of time right here on earth that exists with far advanced space technology? Are there several alien species that exist and one particular "entity" could well be identified as the fallen demonic angels spoken of in the Bible, and led by Satan as their leader? Satan nearly got his dream of a one world government with Hitler until the Supreme Allied Commander of the Allied Expeditionary Force defeated the Nazis. The Supreme Allied Commander of the Military Forces was Dwight D. Eisenhower. Eisenhower was the man Satan wanted to talk to. Satan has visions to become the world's next supreme commander and ruler of Earth. It wasn't long before this 5 star general became President of the United States and Satan wanted to talk to this new Supreme Commander about making a deal with him, the Devil.

Harry Truman was the President in July 1952 when seven UFO's buzzed the White House. America already knew a lot of "alien activity existed all over the world", but Eisenhower did not answer the call when Satan buzzed the Whitehouse wanting to talk with the newly elected president. The only "future" Satan could see was Eisenhower would easily win the election and he was in a hurry to meet with this new elected president who commanded all of Europe's military forces and now has been elected as president. During two separate weekends, seven UFO's were dispatched to buzz and surround the White House. During the night of July 19, 1952 at 11:41 p.m., 7 unidentified UFO's surrounded the White House and played cat and mouse with American

Air Force pilots of the F-94 fighter jets, and the saucers easily outmaneuvered the fighter jets until 5 a.m. President Harry Truman had already established an ultra secret committee by executive order called Majestic 12 in 1947 to investigate the Roswell UFO crash. However, Truman's Majestic 12 team went on high alert when and the flying saucers sped away at "upwards of 7,000 mph." When the American fighter jets returned for fuel, the UFO's came back and continued to buzz uninterrupted until 5:30 in the morning. The following weekend of July 26, the UFO's returned for another display of technology we knew nothing about. One thing for certain was Satan was growing more than anxious to meet with this Supreme victorious Commander and General of the Armies and newly elected President of the United States.

In the meantime, Truman and his generals were preoccupied explaining to Americas' worried citizens the incidents that occurred in Roswell, NM were a "weather event", "temperature inversion" or a "weather balloon." Everything had become enshrouded in secrecy and Satan was getting tired of waiting, so he came and knocked on the White House door (flying above the roof) enough times that finally, in February 1954, President Eisenhower supposedly met with the aliens. In 1953, Truman couldn't wait to pass the reins of power on to President Eisenhower. It included knowledge of the MJ-12 and Ike was intrigued and extremely interested in the subject of UFO's and ET's and carried a strong belief in life on other planets. It is said that Eisenhower secretly met with the aliens at Edwards Air Force Base in California and Holloman Air Force Base on three separate occasions. The aliens wanted us to stop testing nuclear weapons and wanted peace. Rumors also were that the aliens wanted the public to be told the truth about their existence, then retracted their request and demanded secrecy. In February 1954, Ike was on vacation in Palm Springs and then "disappeared" to have a chipped tooth repaired at Holloman Air Force Base. Our president disappeared from the area of Palm Springs and the news media were busily preoccupied thinking the president had "died of an apparent heart attack" until it was found out that the reason for his disappearance was attributed to a supposed dental visit no one was able to confirm with any certainty. It was reported that Eisenhower "signed" some extraterrestrial/terrestrial, celestial/angelic/demonic agreements with some Nordic dudes and the Greys (the atrociously smelly ones like Mr. Phil Schneider described when he encountered and shot at the Greys, deep down in one of the Deep Underground Military Base System (DUMBS). End of hypothetical scenario.

The science of space tells us if we can see out there 46 billion light years we can mathematically come up with a number that tells us its exact speed. So, what? Does it matter how much more money we need to spend to find out more about our universe? Why? We don't even know if flying saucers and aliens are even real. Heck, I don't even know if my president is real! (pun intended.)

josephusflaviussolo@gmail.com

Chapter 42

"Troy" Means "Gift of God"

A wide variety of Pharmaceuticals failed to cover the most lingering trauma issues I have been left with in life. I began a series of taking small mg. dosages of THC and slowly worked up to almost 5 mg. before I began experiencing its effects. It was a feeling of peaceful relaxation, maybe a sense of mild euphoria like drinking 1 beer or 1 glass of wine as fast as you can. Over time, I have built up a tolerance for 10 and 15 mgs. When I decide to party and enjoy the evening with a peaceful, great feeling that cannot be imitated with alcohol, I might take more.

We all know what the alcohol sugar high produces, but the one who takes THC in a self prescribed, and precise mg. dosage is a completely different person when he or she gets toasted. Anger, cockiness and disrespect does not occur in a person that uses THC. What it does do is help to ease a person's heavy baggage of life and does allow for a deep and positive logical thinking process in a manner that alcohol cannot hold a candle to.

What is a peripheral visionary? It is a person that is capable of capturing fast moving visions that come in from the side, and not necessarily ones that strike the (somatic) visionary nerve head on. I believe the Somatic Nervous System (SNS) is enhanced by the use of THC because it operates and energizes the sensory aspects of the brain. THC seems to accelerate, expand and proliferate afferent neuron activity, (a.k.a. sensory neuron activity). Everyone has the capacity for Instant Fragments of Thought (IFT's). However, not all people are willing or capable of capturing or recognizing these Instant, Fragments of Thought. The speed of the IFT does not linger very far outside the box of normal thought, such that it is.

An example of a Somatic Nervous System is described as: "While walking in a tropical forest, a person has a strong tendency to watch the forest floor for fallen twigs, insects, rocks, snakes or undergrowth." This is normal Somatic Nerve function. However, THC stimulates the sensory aspects of the Somatic Nerve System for instantaneous fragments of thought in such a manner, it enables a persons mind to experience an IFT much more readily. When the SNS is hyper stimulated from the effects of THC, it alerts the Central Nervous System within milliseconds.

Some people using THC, ignore the IFT's, or don't care to listen or see the sensory inspiration when it occurs. Some IFT's are incredibly innovative and come to one's mind with great speed. So, have a notepad handy to document the instant thought before it leaves. I perceive IFT's as an event precipitated by a billion of fast moving neurons that spark all around the somatic sensory system, rendering the person capable of an Instantaneous Fragment of Thought, (IFT). The key is to be open to identify the IFT the instantaneous moment it occurs. After some relaxation and open mindedness, the IFT's will come, so be ready for them. I feel the brain can be taught to receive numerous incoming IFT's. So, does everyone have the ability to manage and record the thought when it comes in at light speed? Yes, I feel it is possible by training the mind to be prepared for a quick capture of that thought and be sure to record the event on paper. The instantaneous nature of IFT moments do not last seconds or minutes. IFT's would be best described as an event that occurs within a fraction of a moment of time, but likely no longer in duration. When it happens, you must be open, relaxed and ready. Some IFT's will astound you. IFT's are not bad or cruel, greedy, lofty or evil. But, I would never take THC without a doctor's approval first.

I have discussed and described the meaning of an Instant Fragment of Thought to many of my friends who use THC on a frequent basis. All agreed they have experienced instantaneous fragments of thought on a regular basis as well. One man, in particular was a person I deliberately made friends with. Troy is a true friend and we are grounded in our trust in one another. When this country completely loses it, I want him in my foxhole. I knew this man from the start. During our friendship we are free to talk openly about any subject and during the time Troy is using THC, he comes up with Instantaneous Fragments of Thought (IFT) that astound me. He has not read my book yet, but nearly every subject content he brings up during deep conversation comes to him by way of IFT and can only make me wonder if he is somehow, reading my un-published book. Most of his IFT's are topics written in this book! It's re-markable. This man is 20 years younger and there are so many things we have in common, some would think Troy is my son. I was not familiar with his services or what he did as a means of income until one night he shared a story about helping the elderly. His dedication, respect and mo-tives are commendable. His love and compassion for others is exemplary and I wish I were free to explain to you more about this man's heart with-out revealing his identity, but I know he is well respected and loved by many people for the good things he has done for others. I would list him as one of my heroes because he has a heart of love, kindness and respect for others. While there are not many like him, I covet our friendship and I know he has a heart that's seen by God. Scripture tells us man looks on the outside, but God is the only one that sees inside and knows the heart.

When he introduces me to his close friends (i.e. friends of wisdom), he boldly states "he is my friend, he's one of us" without realizing how much those words really mean to me.

In 1966 I was taking a short cut through a large Army staging field. I helped close a bar at Fort Rucker, Alabama and it was around 1 a.m. I did not know there were 20 black men waiting in the darkness to beat the hell out of some white guys that night. All of a sudden out of the darkness many angry black men surrounded us. Their anger and prejudice was apparent and the situation looked very bleak. The Army did not teach us to fight. The Army only taught us to kill, so I knew this would become a deadly confrontation. Before fists started flying, one black man yelled out "leave them alone, man!" "He is my friend, he's one of us!" One of the black soldiers in the crowd remembered me somehow, and diverted a horrible situation.

They let us pass through the dark staging field untouched. Days later, I caught up with the black man who stood up on my behalf and said those words, "he's one of us." Apparently, I had befriended him at some point and he knew the respect and sincerity in my heart. I have no other explanation for what motivated this black man to step forward and stand up for a white man he knew as "friend." I must have been nice to him and talked with him as an equal. I cannot explain this, but 3 months later someone in a very high position of authority (real high), sent me on a mission to fly to Addis Ababa, Ethiopia on a military mission for 2 years so I could learn all about love with my fellow Ethiopian friends. Ironically, we were known as Mapping Mission. Maybe it was God who could see my heart inside and gave me a "Mission" for 2 of the greatest years of my life with black people. My 8 years experience in the military was full of the most wonderful mix of foreign people I had ever met. Love for fellow man abounds everywhere if you are proactively kind and sincere. Of all the countries I have been to, I was never without true friends. My true friends are of all races and colors of the rainbow. You will never see the colors of the rainbow fighting each other, so if you see a black man or black woman, a Vietnamese man or woman an Ethiopian man or woman or any color or combination of race, be sure to be the first color to greet and show friendship towards your fellow man. Our DNA proves we are all related. How have we become such bitter enemies, festered by prejudice, animosity and hatred towards our own humanity? Why is no one bitching about the color red, which pulses through our veins? At least we share that in common and it becomes a moot point.

There is one point that I want to leave with you and it tears at my heartstrings. It's something Troy is and does. Troy can be in mixed races and feel completely comfortable saying "he's one of us." Troy's use of the word "us" is the focus. That is so deep I have trouble wrapping my head around it.

Thank you Troy. Your IFT's are worthy subjects yet to be discussed and I hope we have years to pontificate all of them. I respect you as a man and admire the love you have in your heart for others and the Spirit of God that dwells within you. Sometimes, I feel I am beginning to pass the torch for others to carry on. So, carry on.

Troy and I "found each other." He still thinks he found me first but I was the one that found him and he knows it. We continue to discuss who was first.

Thanks for your true friendship, Troy. The testimony of who you are is a fine example for others to follow. This is why I look up to you and found you first. I do believe you are a Gift of God.

josephusflaviussolo@gmail.com

Chapter 43

WEENIE SEARCH

What happened to the red, white and blue? Remember the America who listened to "Bye, Bye Miss American Pie", known and sung by just about every service man and woman in the 60's and 70's and even today? The American Pie world began with pie all over our faces by the year 2000 or so. Fear and panic reigned with the threat of a total computer shutdown over all of America. This fake news took place because someone declared the sky was falling and the computers' clock of time will reach its peak at the minute the clock hits midnight 2000, and there will be a total shut down of the world's computers. "Fear and panic" struck nearly every American mind based on absolutely nothing at all. The fear suddenly went away when we all found there was never a world wide computer shutdown, "that would devastate all of the inhabitants of this planet!" As a result of fear alone, the political puppet masters quickly identified just how the American mind reacts. Fear was a word bolstered by the fat guy in the Nazi movement standing right there by the side of Hitler. After the end of WWII, the fat guy stood before the Judgment at Nuremburg and boasted again about the word "fear." Later, fat guy Hermann Goering, was smuggled in his prison cell a strychnine pill to escape his earthly judgment only to experience eternal death right after he swallowed. He was known to boast at mankind's ability to be controlled by fear and fear alone. Striking fear and panic in people and countries everywhere is precisely the psychological secret weapon that Nazi Germany extensively used. The corrupt exclusive Nazi's delighted in the money, power, fame and greed factors, never fearing anything except what size of a building they would need to hold their money in. While the world looked away from the killing of Jews and other races, the masses ignored their plight. Instead, those people of many countries that could "care less" shared in the guilt and blame. America was one of them. History speaks of the countless Hebrew and other refuges who stood aboard ships begging for freedom and safety, while America closed its big Red, White and Blue stripes, painted them yellow and turned their backs on humanity and ordered the immigrating freedom seeking ships away from American soil. Savagery flourished in all corners of the world, while the hatred raged on, the ships full of immigrants could only wonder why America wasn't free like they thought it was.

The thought of freedom is what motivated my father and thousands of others to join the Army during WWII. He knew it was his "heart felt duty" as tons of young men like him enlisted or were drafted to fight a battle of good against evil and to uphold freedom. The First Amendment guarantees freedoms concerning religion, expression, assembly, and the right to petition. Has freedom changed its definition because a recent survey of 4,000 Americans, found "we like it", whatever that means. If the First Amendment needs to be amended let's accurately describe the meaning of those five freedoms in detail. Of the five freedoms, the freedom of religion needs a more finite description because I see a lot of political compromise going on. The freedom to assemble in America has been compromised like politicians handing out speeding tickets at the Indy 500. How about that right to petition? What's going on with those politically driven web application owners who choose to ban certain users of the app based upon prejudice is it? Does that act become an exception to our "guaranteed freedoms" in the First Amendment? The one I really want to have a clear description of is our "freedom of expression." I hope I have the right to express an expression towards political corruption cause you may not like it. I am no part of the "we like it" clan. We need an honest, proficient law making group interested in truth and fairness instead of an old pack of brainless weasel weenies feeding on fame, power, greed and corruption. Don't do what the hungry Egret does while looking down into a pool of small fish. Freedom is not just another word for nothing left to do. Freedom needs a new meaning.

FACTOID: The ball of it all. Dimples in a golf ball extends flight an average of 60 yards beyond the distance of a smooth, round golf ball. So, who knows why?

josephusflaviussolo@gmail.com

Chapter 44

BE KIND TO ANIMALS

I did not research why we should or shouldn't be kind to our animals. My kindness of love comes from the heart. Some people don't have those units, and the heartless are seen everyday where we shop and go. I don't know how many are out there, nor do I have an opinion about them one-way or the other. However:

It was in 2015 or so, when we bought a nice country house in the pine trees of Northeastern Texas and my wife and I decided to live a little dream on 3 ½ acres with 200 tall pine trees and a fish pond. Out on a country dirt road one day I spotted what I thought was a puppy and when I stopped the truck and called, he wagged that tail as hard as any Fox Terrier could. I always tried to keep a can of dog food in the truck, so I found one and laid its contents down near a section of asphalt road and it was apparent this little guy had not eaten in a while. The road was in the middle of nowhere, so I lifted his big tummy and pushed the puppy over to the other seat. I'm pretty sure he had a smile on his face, happy over a full tummy and as we rolled down the road, he fell sound asleep. As we all know, the rest of the story is equal to all the loving times you remember of your own precious dogs and cats that left for a heavenly home early or when they grew old and sick, knowing they would see you again in another place. Evangelist Billy Graham felt our loved animals would be seen again in heaven.

So, after loving that old dog Timber so, so very much. After all the dedication and respect he showed me. After he taught me how to play ball for so many months and the years after protecting our little ranch for so many nights of freezing and snow, some young driver in a dirty white pickup ran over Timber's lower spine and legs, causing a death sentence for one of the very best friends I have ever had in my life. Eyes blurred by tears, I could barely see the lock on the gate, knowing what I was going to have to do to the one loving ball of fur that first picked me to experience his abounding love for 2 years. What depth of love is this, that we experience when owning a dog or a cat, who has loved us unconditionally? The pet who always listened when you talked and never once telling you he or she is having a bad day? I could tell Timber the tallest of tales, while reminding him the rabbits and squirrels are our friends as we both gazed out over the pasture. Timber would lay up on the bench as close as he could get to me and slowly drift off to sleep so many times I cannot remember. He never came to work late and managed the perimeter like a good trooper. I could sit and talk to Timber anytime and he would always quietly tilt his head and listen. He was my shadow and in my shadow.

When I got to the house I came out with my 12 gauge shotgun and said goodbye because Timber was in agony and I just couldn't bear the thought of the excruciating pain he was in. I don't know how many times I cried and told him I was sorry and I loved him so much but he didn't reply because he never complained. I still cry over how much I miss him and when I see him in some of my old pictures I will never forget that I was the one who had to make the decision to put Timber out of his misery.

It's been 5 years and I still haven't recovered the loss of my partner, my shadow, my friend. I know there are thousands of good people out there who feel the same way about their pets. To those who were and are the loving, kind owners and caretakers, I commend you greatly. Let's all be kind to animals. And, let's all be kind to each other, too with a reminder to love your animals, because our character traits might revisit us someday on a giant screen of life for all to see how abusive we may have been towards animals, our children and spouses, friends and workplace. So, watch out.

La discipline engendre le respect, le respect engendre l'amour
J. Flavius Solo

Then again, maybe it's time for me to sweep my front porch and make sure my glass house has no broken panes. josephusflaviussolo@gmail.com

FACTOID: Gray wolves. There just has to be a more effective means of controlling wolves eating sheep and other rancher's animals. One way is not to leave the wolves to be shot and suffer or laying in a trap with broken bones or deliberately run over by a truck. Logic and compassion tells me that if a surgical castration procedure were set into place, there would be a program of safely trapping at least ¾ of the male population and surgically castrating them. After release, the sterile male will no longer produce any more young pups in the pack. And, ¾ of the population would be reduced in no time at all. Killing and trapping our animals is not the answer, but logical sane sterilization practices could prevail if that were possible. If the Grey Wolf population becomes reduced too much, then reduce the castration program to ½ instead of ¾ of the pack. As in the case of the Golden Eagles, the population of eagles would increase by replacing the hens with younger females who aren't so bitchy. We might even try that procedure to increase the endangered California Condor population! (lol, but you see my point, I hope.)

josephusflaviussolo@gmail.com

Chapter 45

A HERO DOG NAMED BERNIE

Many years have past since the story of an old English sheep dog was told. Somewhere high in the slopes of France was the snow of a lifetime. By the time he got there in his 4 wheel drive, the anticipation of skiing a day on the tops of new, white velvet snow from the night before, was overwhelming. He couldn't wait to get on the chair lift, and ride that beautiful pristine slope again this year. As he gazed out over the vista, it was easy to become overcome with joy. Who could ask for a more perfect day as he stood at the top of France's most beautiful slopes, and being the first to ski this virgin snow? It was beyond his imagination or the expense it took to get him there. Whooooooooosh, as the white powder billowed. The skis lifted, glided and danced, with the soft velvety spray of those hard waxed surfaces. He twisted in delight as he made his way, gliding down the mountain in the velvet snow, making zig zags of every kind, and then it happened. The entire shelf of the mountain ridge gave way, and the avalanche began tumbling down behind, a massive wall of snow gaining speed, and overcoming the skier. As the mountain of snow tumbled, and crushed all things in its path, it left the skier deeply buried somewhere beneath the rocks and snow. The French Survival Team responded immediately, knowing that rescue time was essential to ensure the survival of the skier. They brought out long rods to probe the depths, and with them were four Search and Rescue dogs. The dogs were big and husky dogs of every color, and this wasn't their first survival trek. Along with the three rescue dogs was an older Saint Bernard, who had seen many seasons of his days on the ridges, sniffing for a clue as to where a lost skier might be. The dog's eyes and hearing were beginning to fade with age, and the team feared this trip could be his last. But Bernie, the old Saint Bernard, drew in all of his strength to show the team he was still in the game, while barking with the others in a cacophony of excitement, anxious to begin their search. Once again, old Bernie breathed deeply in anticipation of the search, and saved his strength for the rescue. This old dog was a veteran, but his days of rescue missions would soon end, and he longed to give his old, tired, bones a rest, and retire on someone's front porch somewhere, where it wasn't so cold. Somehow, Bernie knew this rescue mission would be his last.

The team and four dogs quickly spread out as the men with their long rods lined up in single file, and began probing the depths, hoping for the feel of a human body. All of the dogs fanned out as the old sheep dog ran to a distant area, and worked in a large clockwise fashion until he picked up a scent. After 30 minutes of sniffing and digging, the scent became stronger until finally, Bernie went into super strength mode, and began digging furiously, with every ounce of his being. Finally, those old frosted hairy eyes of his barely made out what looked like a blue ski jacket hood, and the man was buried deep. The dog's instinct was to dig down around the man's head, and down deep enough to pull the man from his freezing prison. Bernie was highly trained and instantly knew what was expected of him. Bernie stretched those old muscles one more time, and continued digging, and continued to dig with the fervor of a John Deere backhoe. The snow was filthy, and riddled with rocks of every size as the dog struggled to dig with those big paws, and the small rocks cut and tore at the bottoms of Bernie's front feet, as stains of red blood began spattering all over the dirty snow. The dog was exhausted from pulling, and nearly out of breath, and then tugged even more as he pulled the man to the top of the snow, nearly collapsing and out of breath. Bernie could tell the man was freezing cold, as he crawled over to the man, and laid his warm, bloody, furry old tired body over the man to try to keep him warm. In the far distance Bernie could finally hear the other dogs, and men responding to the scene. When the other dogs and the men arrived, they quickly moved old Bernie to the side to rest, and loaded the survivor on the cot. The other dogs already knew that Bernie was lying there dead, and bleeding in the dirty snow.

Before the rescue team got to the scene, the man had regained his consciousness, only to look up to see a large furry animal of some kind, lying on top of him, and certain all the blood in the snow was his. In the confusion, the skier thought the furry animal was eating his flesh, and he felt in great danger, and reached down for his survival knife only to plunge the sharp knife deep into the side of Bernie, killing the very one that saved him. The old Saint Bernard gave his life to save the life of a man caught in an avalanche, and the skier never knew it. Over the many years of telling this story, I become reminded at times, over the sadness, thinking that an old English sheep dog named Bernie, was such a tragedy that he had given every ounce of his strength, and even die to save that man.

More years of time has passed since I thought of this story, when I realized my very best Hero, Jesus Christ gave up His life, on a cross, just for me. For the first 36 years of my life, I plunged the knife of rejection deeply into the side of the God because I didn't know Him. My biggest obstacle was I didn't appreciate being preached to by friends, and others. People didn't need to know I knew very little about the bible, or knew little about why there was a New Testament or Old Testament. Then, one day, I had a conversation with an old Christian sage, who suggested I demonstrate the authenticity of the bible by researching the prophecies. Sopped up with a scientific mind, I launched myself on a new quest to find out about prophetic scriptures, specifically, the Bible's accuracy, and fulfillment of the prophecies. Ironically, I found that nearly 97% of the New Testament prophecies, and about 95% of the Old Testament prophecies had already been fulfilled with 100% accuracy. I found the prophecies were scientifically, geographically, and historically accurate. I found it acutely interesting what the prophets had to say, and learned more about the prophecies, that spanned over time, even 1,200 years before, and being fulfilled with 100% accuracy, 100% of the time. I read the Gospel of John, and learned about my Savior, who gave his life for mankind, but an element of thought lingered deep in my mind, as I was not convinced the Bible was the true source of scripture until the Bible prophecies authenticated the Word of God is without error. Were you aware the Bible challenges us to search the prophecies? Otherwise, God would have never told us how to identify a false prophet. We are warned about the false prophets, and the words were given to us as to how to identify a false prophet. The prophecies must come to pass with 100% accuracy, 100% of the time without error. A false prophet is one who espouses future events that do not occur.

This is not a sermon. What it is though, is that I respect all other religions. Research (i.e. reading and studying the truth), is the key to knowledge. If you believe in something else, or another God, you might want to take a look at their prophecies. Paying attention doesn't cost a thing, and yet it's mans' worst earthly downfall.

For those who disagree, let's intellectually dance on the keypad.

josephusflaviussolo@gmail.com

Chapter 46

———✎———

GONDAR, ETHIOPIA

High above the Road to Gondar, Homer slowly eased the big DeHaviland U-1 Otter north towards the old city of Gondar as mothers ran out of their tukuls below, and countless children waved their arms to greet and see the new sight in the skies. One could feel the cooler temperatures as we climbed even higher to cross the mountains headed towards an old airstrip on the other side. At least that's what Homer called it as we descended near Adi Remoz, while looking for this "runway" somewhere out there. We both recognized the reddish colored faint dirt road runway in the middle of nowhere Africa, and easily touched down in the soft red billowing cloud of dirt, leaving a trail of red dust behind. Our mission was to secure as many empty 55 gallon barrels we could fit in the Otter aircraft. The area was flat all around us as we climbed out of the seats making our way off the plane and down into red dirt. Desolate and red was the soil and it took nothing to kick a cloud dust into the air. Ethiopia was an amazing country and its history is phenomenal. The people were poor and lived in small huts comprised of sticks and mud that would likely be destined as the only "home" they would ever know. I stood gazing at my surroundings of dirt and didn't see any evidence of anyone else wanting to live in such a place. Homer suddenly broke into my deep thoughts and offered me water before we round up the barrels and hydrated in the 120-degree oven of hot dusty red dirt. I felt comfortable in my dirty white t-shirt, a pair of cut off fatigues and an old pair of combat boots that must have been left behind when the British were run out of the country by the Nazi tanks during WWII. Most barrels were an easy find but we needed just three more to make it 14. The other barrels were scattered across the plain, lying on their sides awaiting the next wind to blow them to a new destination. Homer walked out one direction and I took a path towards a lonely barrel I spotted about 200 yards away. It was really getting hot and I was anxious to get back to the plane and fly upwards to grab some high altitude cooler air, but that dirty old barrel was the only thing keeping me from that pleasurable thought.

When I got behind the barrel and gave it a swift kick towards the plane I was pretty sure it was my last day on this planet. This long brown thing crawled out from under the barrel and tried to run up my leg! I was a young rooster of a man and whatever the hell it was, I was on my way to the Olympic run of my life and nearly out of breath, I looked back and this thing was chasing me all over the place! Those old combat boots were running faster than I could keep up, but there was no way this thing was going to catch up with me. I darted every way I could screaming like a little girl (I think. But of course that memory is not too clear any longer, and don't bother asking Homer). Every time I tried to stop, the reptile wasn't tired so I ran and I ran, even around large circles of red dust.

Well, Homer just stood there and watched the show as I streaked one way then another, being chased by one of those long Spitting Cobras old Doc Babbit warned us about. The good doctor briefed us when we got in country. He explained about the spitting cobra, the black mamba, puff adder and the Bitis parviocula. I forgot to wear my sunglasses in the event of a cobra encounter, besides I had very little time to look and identify the reptile. It was after I finally ran past that old 55-gallon barrel again when the 2 foot long lizard stopped off at his home and ran under his barrel. I did not realize all he was looking for was his barrel that gave him shade from the sun and a home to live under. My day calmed down when I realized it was not a spitting cobra or any of those other deadly creatures.

When life offers a bad lemon of a day, it's time to figure out how to make some lemonade. I always try to look for a splinter of good in any situation. In this instance, I was able to get a great physical work-out running 2 miles in the hot sun in a continuous cloud of red dust, caused by moving an old 55-gallon barrel that a lizard called home. The best part of the day was Homer had to fly back to Mapping Mission smelling like a urinal. He pissed his pants laughing at me, "the crazy ass who was running in a cloud of red dirt and screaming like a little girl." At the time of my marathon, Homer and the lizard were the only ones that knew he wasn't a spitting cobra. I am sure that barrel is still resting in the red dirt near Adi Remoz even to this day. I never kicked another empty 55-gallon barrel again. I flew home in a beautiful sunset, drinking sweet lemonade and smiling. Even though I too, nearly pissed my pants, it wasn't such a bad day after-all.

josephusflaviussolo@gmail.com

Chapter 47

──◆◆◆──

THE DISAPPEARANCE
OF UNCLE SAM

What happened to the red, white and blue? Remember the America who listened to the song, "Bye, Bye Miss American Pie", known and sung by just about every service man and woman in the 60's and 70's? The American Pie world began with pie all over our faces by the year 2000. Fear reigned with the threat of a total computer shutdown of all America, because someone declared the sky was falling and the computers' clock of time would reach its peak at the minute the clock hit midnight 2000. Fear struck nearly every American mind based on absolutely nothing at all. The fear suddenly went away when we all found there was never a worldwide computer shutdown, "that would devastate all of the habitants of this planet." As a result of fear, the political puppet masters quickly identified just how the American mind reacts. Fear was a word boasted by the fat guy in the Nazi movement standing right there by the side of Hitler. After the end of WWII, the fat guy stood before the Judgment at Nuremburg and boasted about the word "fear." While he waited in jail, The Fat Guy Goering was smuggled in a strychnine pill to escape his judgment of death. That day he stopped laughing about mankind's ability to be controlled by fear and fear alone. Striking fear in people everywhere is precisely the secret weapon that Nazi Germany used extensively. The corrupt exclusive ones delighted in the money and greed factors, never fearing anything except what size of a building they would need to hold their money. While the world toiled, the killing of Jews was ignored by many countries, which could care less. History speaks of the countless Israeli refuges who stood aboard ships begging for freedom and safety, while America closed its big red, white and blue eyes and turned their backs on humanity and ordered the immigrating freedom seeking ships away from American soil, and not to return, as if to say, "you have no home here in America, we reject you." Savagery flourished in all corners of the world, while the hatred raged on. Historical research will confirm it was no secret we were going to be attacked by Japan. Our president was pleased to know the attack was imminent and America would suffer enough to cause all of American citizens to unite and quickly come together for the cause of freedom. At some point, that was when Uncle Sam "caught the first train for the coast" and the military industrial complex was driving the train.

josephusflaviussolo@gmail.com

FACTOID: The USDA states foreign investors own at least 35.2 million acres of U.S. land. Not to worry though, congress will take good care of our interests.

Chapter 48

—————

GOLD, DON'T COUNT ON IT

From 1933 to 1974 you could not have gold unless it was in jewelry. You could not purchase or hold any gold bullion with out a "license". After 1974, the government decided citizens could buy all the gold we wanted, but if you sell as a personal holder, the law limit is $10,000.00 at a time. You can bet after a few of those 10,000-dollar transactions, someone will be investigating you. In a "National Emergency" you can be sure the government will conjure up and have one of those emergencies in the near future—more near than we think. Once a National Emergency takes effect, every one in America will be required to turn in some or ALL of their gold. Once the law takes effect, any American hoarding, holding, hiding, selling or any other clandestine transaction will most likely be found out about because whether it is an offshore account or not. Somebody from the government is coming for your every ounce of gold, or ring (if they choose to do so), chain or watch. It will be illegal to have possession or hide gold from the government. If that law takes place, I fear that every exchange, purchase, trade or any other transaction regarding gold purchases will be very easily found through the information the government already has in its possession. If you bury it, you will only be able to use that gold in black market sales. Owners of gold better be at the top of their game when dealing with gold in the black market or on the streets. Anyone caught owning gold after the declaration of a national emergency will most likely be severely dealt with unless you are one of the exempt "select citizens of politics." You may not get caught up with quickly, but be confident that information in the computer world can be collected on an individual about everything you have ever done on a computer or cell phone and you won't be able to deal very long before being caught. By then, it will probably be a Federal Offense to hold or possess even one ounce of gold. So, my question is, "just who are the people in the U.S. who really think their gold or gold coins or gold jewelry will be anything of value to them after this country declares a "National Emergency"??? Gold will suddenly become worthless to all of us – even – to – possess.

josephusflaviussolo@gmail.com

Chapter 49

———❧———

THE SUN AND CME

Some of us are well aware of the destructive forces from the sun. In the past, large solar eruptions have disrupted cell phones, computers and many other electrical devices. Our magnetosphere surrounds the earth as a protective barrier for coronal mass eruptions, solar storm activity, including many variations of radiation activity as well as meteor protection. Many times, the protective balloon of our magnetosphere becomes blasted by the sun's solar winds, making the front of the protective balloon extremely concave and nearer to the earth. The magnetosphere yields under the intense solar wind, and takes the shape of a giant streamlined teardrop of protection around the earth. As the sun's storm continues to blast the front side of earth's magnetosphere, a giant tail forms on the backside of earth, and makes an unseen tail that some say is 3.5 million miles long.

What is coronal mass ejection? A giant CME event occurred in 1895, known as the "Carrington Event." It caused a disaster in America that I will explain later. For now, let me just say that if America were to be recipient of a Coronal Mass Ejection (CME), at the G5 level,

America could easily lose ALL electrical power for 4 to 10 years. Why? Because all of our electrical grids would shut down and transformers would likely explode, rendering America helpless. All computers, cell phones and vehicles will cease to function. No transportation will exist other than bicycles and gasoline vehicles. Crime will become rampant, gas and food will be scarce. Banks will be closed, clean water will be a problem that will be worse than it now is, and most shallow metal gas lines will erupt in a burst of flames from the effects of the CME, (this information is based upon what some sources claim regarding the destructive forces of a G5 level Coronal Mass Ejection).

Let's meander through this stuff together, and take smaller steps to understand where I am coming from, so we all get a clear understanding. Here are some cosmos 101 subjects, without the use of big words:

Our Sun is a large star. It is the center of our solar system, and all of our planets revolve around the sun, (Galileo spent the rest of his life under house arrest for making that statement. He was convicted of heresy). Our sun is approximately 93 million miles away from planet earth, and light streams from the sun at 186,000 miles per second, (669 million miles per hour) and the light takes about 8 minutes to get here. The second nearest sun from our solar system is Proxima Centauri, which is located about 4.247 light-years away in the southern constellation of Centaurus. Our sun is very large and can fit in about 1 million of our earths. The sun provides for most of the needs of us earthlings and all other life. Robert A. Heinlein wrote a book about the moon being a harsh mistress, but the sun can also be a harsh mistress when its polar field switches poles every 11 years. Switching poles is when the sun's north pole changes polarity from positive to negative, and the south pole of the sun changes from negative to positive. When this happens, the sun can get a nasty, stormy bad attitude, and not behave until another solar cycle visits in 11 more years. Someone has been keeping track of this solar cycle since 1755, naming the first one Solar Cycle 1. We are presently experiencing Solar Cycle 25, which began in

2019, with a potential for peak sunspot activity in 2025. Once an 11 year cycle gets 1/3 into its phase, the sun can get real nasty and gush out its hot, radioactive plasma at much larger proportions and more frequently.

Solar Storm: A disturbance on the sun that can cause damage to power grids on earth, and may affect the entire solar system. The NOAA Geomagnetic Storm Scale is numbered as G1 to G5. A G5 event can be severe. Scientists estimated the Carrington Event of 1895, a G5.

Solar Flare: Is known as a burst of radiation. An intense eruption of electromagnetic radiation is typically harmless, unless you were living near Quebec in March 13, 1989, when a geomagnetic storm caused a nine-hour outage of Hydro-Quebec's electricity transmission system, including some other recorded instances in history.

NOAA Space Weather Scales: R, S, and G:

R Scale: The R scale has to do with radio blackouts. R1 is low and an R5 is high, depicting severity. For example R1 is minor, but can cause intermittent loss of radio contact. However, an R5 on the sunlit side of earth will be extreme, and cause a complete blackout of all HF Radio and navigation for hours.

S Scale: (Solar Radiation Storms.) Designated by NOAA the S scale is numbered 1 through 5. An S1 is minor and can have impact of HF Radio in the Polar Regions. An S5 is extreme and causes unavoidable high radiation to astronauts and all aircraft flying at high altitudes, such as our commercial aircraft, which may be exposed to a radiation risk if flown into these sectors. (I would hope the FAA is tracking high radiation areas in the sky to make sure all commercial flights in the world are required to circumvent the threat area to avoid an S3, S4 or S5 "radiation risk" because I plan to fly in one of your aircraft soon.)

G Scale: (Geomagnetic Storms.) Designated by NOAA, the G scale represents the strength and severity of geomagnetic storms, and is numbered 1 through 5. A G1 is minor and some power grid fluctuations can occur at this level. Migratory animals can be affected at the G1 to G5 levels. A G5 storm is severe and can cause widespread voltage control issues, some grid systems could experience complete blackouts and transformers may sustain damage. However, according to other sources, a G5 has the potential of another Carrington Event that first occurred in 1895. (So, what are the emergency procedures if a G5 or G6 were to occur? Do we have any?)

Solar Flares: Solar flares are often associated with solar magnetic storms known as Coronal Mass Ejection (CME). Solar flares are classed as the smaller A class, and B, C, M and X class, which is severe. The energy produced by a solar flare is a million times more powerful than the energy from a volcanic explosion here on earth. The most powerful solar flare occurred in 2003, during the last solar maximum with so much force, the monitor sensors cut out at about X17, and was later estimated to be about X45! The ionizing radiation released during a solar flare includes x-rays and gamma rays. Solar flares increase during the maximum period of the solar cycle.

Coronal Mass Ejection: A CME is a gigantic hot plasma ring, blown out into space, up to a million miles away from the surface of the sun. In some cases, the CME hot plasma can separate and reconnect, causing a force of energy released comparable to a billion hydrogen bombs. Some CME activity from the sun can travel outward at speeds that take only 15 to 18 hours to reach earth.

Carrington Event: Two astronomers in London, were checking out the sun and looking at solar flares. It was 28 August 1859, when they saw a series of sun spot formations that danced and intermingled with the magnetic influences of the sun. For one of the first times a Coronal Mass Ejection (CME), was seen. Whether it was one giant massive CME or two in conjunction is not known. The two observers had no idea what that event was, but they described it with factual drawings and data, and we know now it was a big kahuna CME! Some say G5, or.... +? Seventeen hours later, America took a direct hit from the effects of the CME. In 1895, Telegraph systems all across North America and parts of Europe caused electrical shock to its operators. Lines sparked in some populated areas and started a few telegraph pole fires. A web source states "set fire to telegraph stations," and history warns us "this (Carrington Event), may be something that will occur much more frequently." Drawings from an account in 1770, confirmed that China and parts of Japan were affected by a sunspot super storm twice the size of the Carrington sun-spots. Super storms of similar amplitudes were recorded in 1872 and 1921, so it seems we might be overdue. However, a big, big blastitude of a solar storm just missed our earth in 2012! I mean, just missed! This one had the potential of exceeding that of the Carrington Event, and we were lucky. So, what if we weren't lucky? No cars after a short time, no electricity, no cell phone contact, no water, no food no school (yaaay!). How long would it take for American Citizens to enter another civil war should a giant G5 devastate America?

Some sources believe if we receive a direct hit in America, we'll know about it 17 hours before it inflicts its damage. That would be a good time to get your shopping done, fill the tank with gas, call, text, twitter, and face book all your friends, eat 2 or 3 nice hot meals, take the kids out of school, purchase several bottles of wine, fill the bathtub with drinking water, while building several Faraday Cages to protect your car, computers, cell phones, yourself and family etc., etc., and sit back with Merle Haggard on the yoyo tube and sing along with his song, "We'll all be drinking that free Bubble Up, and eating that Rainbow Stew", until it hits.

After it hits. All hell could easily break loose on this planet. We could be in a 4 to 10 year shutdown of all electrical grids. Some experts have said that all sub-surface natural gas lines could even explode; now that's crazy.

In the interim, I am honestly more concerned about the solar radiation levels we are getting from the sun on a daily basis. The sun produces Visible Light, Ultraviolet Light, Infrared, Radio Waves,

X-rays and Gamma Rays. Some forms of solar radiation like UV-B is on the increase, due to the ozone depletion, and is causing more cases of sunburn, which can lead to cancer and adversely impact the body's immune system. Ultraviolet A radiation can cause damage to our DNA. Even though the earth is surrounded by a protective outer shield known as the "magnetosphere", harmful UV-A, UV-B and Gamma radiation can still penetrate through the protective magnetosphere shield and adversely affect the human body's immune system. It seems to me that the National Oceanic and Atmospheric Administration would ask the National Weather Service to include information about all harmful radiation bursts from the sun. I am not advocating we all should wear a dosimeter or carry a Geiger counter, but it would be nice if we were better informed about our absorption of radioactive solar activity and whether our children should wear hats while outdoors on high UVI solar energy days. For now, the American public has no idea where on this earth the next solar energy splash will hit. We have no daily reports or data of potential UV, X-ray or Gamma doses that could slip through the magnetosphere. I am very concerned about this when it was discovered that the National Weather Service waited until 1958 before Americans were ever told, or warned about tornadoes. The reason we weren't forewarned about tornadoes? They, (NWS) didn't want us Americans to "panic."

One source on the web offers what to do during a Carrington Event:

1. Prepare ahead of time. The main threat will be a black out and darkness at night.
2. Save and ration your food. Grocery stores may run out of food quickly.
3. Secure your house. Know who your friends are.
4. Don't travel.
5. Hide a wad of cash. Forget gold and silver, heathen friends know you've got it.
6. Pray.

In 1970, some scientists analyzed and forecasted an immense heat event "will occur" at the earth's inner core and induce a migration of hot lava liquids of energy flowing towards the ice layers in the Polar Regions, causing weakness or destruction of earth's magnetic field. If this is happening, scientists back in 1970 were saying that because we already have lost about 15% of our magnetic field strength up to the year 1970 (more recent percentages are now stating it's really 9 or 10%, however, the magnetic field has a "weak spot that is expanding.") These scientists believed in 100 years, from 1970, the magnetic fields would weaken to the point, that we will have no more protection from our protective magnetosphere. So, the math tells us if these scientists were/ are correct, us earthlings have a potential 48 years to go before the possibility of losing our magnetosphere completely. So, 2070 is the big day? Is this why Elon Musk is so focused on transporting masses (of the rich and elite people) to other planets? His rocket corporation surpassed the ingenuity and intelligence capability over all other rocket companies. He has a staff of great engineers, who come up with the ideas for space travel, not bound or suppressed by a government con-tract or political oversight (I hope). Elon's engineers and science team are a conglomeration of the finest aerospace engineering minds on this earth and I would bet Elon listens to their ideas and makes some of them reality. This may also explain why Elon has made electric cars. Isn't he also owner of the Boring Company?

Assuredly, the method of some of Elon's madness does have a mo-tive. Think about it. Why else would he form Space X, own a massive laser boring machine and build electric cars?

I'm thinking the future of mankind will be living in massive un-derground complexes, not because we want to, but because we have to. It is possible that in 2070, this earth's magnetic field could dissipate to the point that a genuine Global Warming will occur (however, I think it may have already started.) Remember in the 1990's, when the push was on to change out all your bulbs and go fluorescent to cut down on global warming? More rabbit trails, more lies. I feel hopeful that Elon

Musk is a genuine visionary and I believe he has already had confidential communications with members of congress, if not the president. I do not think it a conspiracy if the human population is not told in 48 years we may be living underground, or on the moon, or on mars. Otherwise, what is all the hurry to get to Mars and explore the moon again?

Once the magnetosphere weakens, every kind of cancerous ionizing radiation from the sun will strike the surface of the earth with massive blasts of solar winds, cosmic debris and constant bombardment of lethal radiation to destroy most flora and fauna on earth's surface. However, all will not be lost because of the genius mind of Elon and his fellow engineers and scientists. The best part is Elon and his team will already know how to convert surface radiation storms into a source of perpetual free energy for all who live down below. Free energy, because he's that caliber of man. Or is he?

I find it interesting to note the Parker Solar Probe was launched to a destination orbit of the sun in 2018. It replaced the old Helios 2 spacecraft that orbited the sun 27 million miles off the sun's surface. The new Parker Solar Probe is even closer now, estimated at 3.87 million miles from the sun and will provide far more accurate data on the sun's lethal cosmic activity.

All the while, life will continue beneath the ground. We already have 120 Deep Underground Military Bases (D.U.M.B.S.), protected far beneath the surface of the earth with a complex network of underground freeways that crisscross all over America. Deep in the giant tunnels, the air remains clean as day-to-day duties continue, because they're using electric vehicles and electric oxygen filtration generators as needed or for perpetuity, (or is this news to you?).

The year 2070 is a long ways away for me to worry about........... and yet, 1970 wasn't so long ago. In fact, Elon Musk was born in 1971 and that wasn't so long ago either, right?

josephusflaviussolo@gmail.com

Author's comment:

I am thinking Josephus has gotten a lot of stuff out of his system. Me too, because during the multi year process it took me in the writing of this book I have been able to realize I can't possibly save the world. What it has done to me personally, is it has caused me to change. It takes just one person to start change:

1. And love one another.
2. And be respectful and don't lie to your children.
3. And Love your wife and family – that's all you've got.
4. And be a living example of goodness and kindness.
5. And help others.
6. And research because the truth will set you free.
7. And have a forgiving heart. Even for those repenting, stinking politicians if that were possible.
8. Strive to become an accomplished epistemologist.

For me, the book has been a 10 or more year combination of subjects I wanted to research and write about. I hope there were some good stories, but Josephus portrays a dooms day world. Unfortunately, many agree a dooms day will occur. Politics, hatred, war, racial prejudice, killings, another civil war, disease, pestilence, panic, darkness, suffering, nuclear radiation fears, UFO's, the moon and mars, solar mass eruptions, earthquakes, tornadoes and sun G5's are on the way!

I am not worried in the least about a nuclear war destroying the earth. I learned to let worry, worry for it's self. The truest hero I could ever have is in another Son. The Son of God. Jesus Christ died on a cross as a sacrifice so we could have everlasting life. Sins died for all of us when His blood fell. Jesus became the sacrificial Lamb on our behalf. He bore the sins of the world – including your sins. So, years ago, I accepted God's free gift of everlasting life. Times in this world are changing so rapidly I am amazed at the technological advances we have made over these last 74 years. Politicians have remained corrupt, murder and rape is on the rise lurking everywhere, our drinking waters are polluted, our air is polluted, schools have radically changed and life is way different than it was a few short decades ago. I am not getting out of touch with anyone challenging my mind in good conversation, but you younger ones are beginning to ignore the older wise ones and assume elderly counsel is not worth the effort. In my case, I am not out of touch at all because Jesus touched me with the promise of the free gift of Grace a long time ago. In the meantime, respect your elders and thank you for taking time out of your life to enter a part of mine.

In times of depression, teach your mind to focus on love, laughter, respect and humor. Read a good book, watch an old movie you love and have seen 3 times already. Be an example of respect and you will get respect in return. Get in touch with your mom and dad or brothers and sisters and tell them how much you love them. Call a friend you know, trust and respect – that's why "friends" are here on this planet. Seek out sage intelligent, positive minded friends and spend some time talking with them and keep your trials and tribulations on hold in conversation to seek out how you can help the one who (I am sure) will have more troubles than your own. By careful listening, you might be the one that was appointed by the Spirit of God to be in on a 2 way conversation that both of you need to hear. Problems that try to steal our joy abound in an uncertain world. Don't let it happen to you. Hold your head high, trust that a living, loving and ever present God is standing right next to you and remember when God seems far away it was us that moved. I have heard that cliché' for years, we've all have experienced strife and tragedy in life. Keep up the Spirit of love and look for the joy and good in each and every person you know. Trust in others until you learn otherwise. For the heathens, avoid them and remain respectful of anyone who does not understand joy and yearn for logic, understanding and love they may have to offer, even if some people you know are stuck on stupid (blind to ignorance, respect and reason).

For those that attempt to take you to anger in any situation, use you intelligent mind by replying and remaining respectful of the subject instead of matching their ignorance or level of anger. By example, help others to learn to respect others in their opinionated stance. Respond to all with respect, honesty and integrity, and be the bigger person who can offer joy, logic and love. Respect those you love. Don't ever forget that. Love and respect your mother and dad as your Father in heaven loves you. Be nice to your Guardian Angels. Guardian Angels are commissioned to watch over you. Indeed, they are watching and listening and will remain by your side until the glory of eternity and God's Angels carry you away into the presence of an almighty God that may tell you, "well done my child." Keep your eyes open in heaven because you will see those who have gone before you. It is extremely hard sometimes to tread the waters of life, but in the meantime, be an example to others so they might learn to love and respect you. Long for the vision that our true joy in life is achieved in spending eternity in the presence of Our Lord and Savior, Jesus Christ. Expect to be united with all Christians in heaven. If you feel you are missing out, read the Book of John and realize the promises or seek out the wisdom of others who know the Word of God. I am always available, but I fall short every day and may not be a perfect example. However, life in the sandbox of reality will never get better and I can hear the not so distant dirge music of the 3 Musketeers of Evil closing in on the precious souls of humanity, to ravage all that he can in a dance of eternal, perpetual tormented existence of lost souls to commune forever, with the 3 Musketeers of Evil, known as Satan, the anti-Christ and the False Prophet.

FACTOID: If a lit candle were placed near a wall, you would easily see the shadow of the candle on the wall, yet the flame of light has no shadow. Darkness cannot overcome light. Darkness flees from the light. God says He is the Light of the World. Believe in Him and you can be saved. Some people tell me it is impossible for them to believe anything based on faith. Sitting in a chair is based on "faith." Do we all inspect each leg of the chair before sitting?

FACTOID: Our planet's magnetosphere endures all of the solar wind. Solar winds can reach up to more than 800 kilometers per second. A solar wind stream at 372 miles per second will blast our outer protective shield of the magnetosphere at a speed of 1,339,200 miles per hour.

josephusflaviussolo@gmail.com

Visit: www.Research-Solo.com for more articles

Thank you for your time to read and research. Look for my new book, "Dammit Billy", in summer 2023.

www.ingramcontent.com/pod-product-compliance
Lightning Source LLC
Chambersburg PA
CBHW070911270326
41927CB00011B/2528